MW00651650

The Data-Centric Revolution

Restoring Sanity to Enterprise Information Systems

Dave McComb

Technics Publications

Published by:

2 Lindsley Road
Basking Ridge, NJ 07920 USA
https://www.TechnicsPub.com

Edited by Lauren McCafferty
Cover design by Lorena Molinari

First Printing 2019

Copyright © 2019 by Dave McComb

ISBN, print ed.   9781634625401
ISBN, Kindle ed.   9781634625418
ISBN, ePub ed.   9781634625425
ISBN, PDF ed.   9781634625432

Library of Congress Control Number: 2019905464

Dedicated to Addie and Eli for their inspiration

Prelude

This book is the first part of a trilogy to follow <u>Software Wasteland</u>. In <u>Software Wasteland</u>, we detailed how bad the current state of the art of application software development is. We offered some tactical advice for reducing some of the worse of the excess.

This book began as the companion book; the "what to do instead" book. But as I started writing it, I realized that there were three audiences not well-served with a single volume.

So, we now have the companion trilogy:

- <u>The Data-Centric Revolution</u> (this volume). Targeted at the executives who will have to champion this movement within each of their firms.

- <u>The Data-Centric Pattern Language</u>. A set of over 100 patterns, presented in the style that Christopher Alexander made famous. The data modelers and ontologists who will design this future state will find this volume most useful. This future is enough different from the present, and old habits die hard, so the second volume is to help designers avoid the temptation to backslide.

- <u>The Data-Centric Architecture</u>. Early adopters have been building their own architecture to support their Data-Centric implementations. We're going to take what we have learned from them and our own experience to construct a blueprint to allow enterprises to adopt this approach as their own, or for enterprising software entrepreneurs to build the platforms of tomorrow. You cannot implement the systems we're talking about in this volume with the architecture you have now. The good news is that this next generation architecture is far simpler than the ones you've been dealing with, and you may be able to reuse many components of the architecture you have now.

Before we start, I'm going to make two apologies, and then retract them. There are two aspects of this book that you may not like, I understand that. At the same time and after a lot of reflection, I don't think I could get the point across without them.

The first apology is for getting too technical in a volume for executives. But what we've noticed is the early proponents of this approach have embraced the technical differences that this approach enables and requires. We've noticed the successful executives have been the ones that embrace enough of this technology to stand up to critics and naysayers. This isn't a simplistic endeavor where you'll be able to get away with simply asking "for the ROI." You won't need to know how to build an ontology yourself, but you will need to know enough to be apprised of what the rest of your team is doing.

The second apology is for the grandiosity of this. As you will soon see, the tone of this is not that this is the next great technology, or that this is an incremental improvement that you can add to your existing repertoire. A very large industry stands in your way, if you take this up. This requires a lot of people changing the way they think, and people need incentive to change. Your firm will need to change the way they think about sharing information. I harp on paradigm change because I think it's essential to have an idea of the challenges that may lie ahead.

So, there you have it. I'm aware of these two flaws in this book. I'm aware that I am subjecting you to this. I apologize for that.

And I retract my apology. I couldn't think of another way to make the points as forcibly as I think is deserved. I hope you can cut me some slack; I made it as short as I could.

Thank you for picking this up. Welcome to the revolution.

Contents

CHAPTER 1
The Data-Centric
Movement

We are at a turning point in the way we manage
enterprise information. Every year the amount of data
available to enterprises doubles, while the ability to
effectively use it decreases. We're spending 3-8% of gross
revenue on application systems that are frustratingly
hard to change at a time when the pace of change needs
to increase. Executives lament their legacy systems, but
projects to replace them end up with moon shot budgets
and rarely succeed.

There is a way out. It is not a technology quick fix. It
requires discipline and understanding that we must view
the entire landscape of enterprise IT through a different
lens. We call this lens the "Data-Centric approach."

As we detail in <u>Software Wasteland,</u> the prevailing mindset for managing enterprise information systems is the "application-centric approach." In the application-centric approach, business problems beget projects that beget application systems. It doesn't matter whether the application system is built, bought or implemented as a service. It doesn't matter what technology is employed. Each additional application, encouraged through the application-centric mindset, creates and manages yet another data model. Over time the result of this approach leads to thousands of applications and therefore thousands of complex data models. Rather than improving access to important information this approach has been steadily eroding it, as the multiplication and variety of models obscures understanding, unnecessarily increases the cost of integration and increases the cost of change. The more firms double down on the application-centric approach, the more stuck they become.

There is a way out: the "Data-Centric approach." It is not something you can buy. It is something you must do. It requires first seeing the landscape and the problems differently, and then having the discipline to change course.

This will not be an easy or rapid transition. Many firms will never make the transition.

In many ways this is comparable to the second stage of the industrial revolution when small stand-alone electric motor-driven machines displaced centralized steam and crankshaft-driven workstations.

As Brian Arthur points out in The Nature of Technology,[2] it was obvious as early as 1880 that new electric motors would transform the industrial revolution, but this transition took over 40 years to play out. There is a parallel here between the transition from steam to electricity and the transition from application-centric to Data-Centric methods. It was not lack of technology that slowed the transition from steam to electricity, just as it is not a lack of technology that prevents the transition from application-centric to Data-

---

[1] Courtesy https://bit.ly/2VNPkX1.

[2] Brian Arthur, The Nature of Technology, https://amzn.to/2GtevZT.

Centric methods. One of the things that held back the
steam to electricity transition (and will likely slow it for
the transition to Data-Centric) was a tight-knit network
of experts who reinforced the status quo.

If you wanted to build a factory in the 1880s, you needed
to hire architects experienced with building factories. At
the time, the biggest problem for architects to solve was
the stress that the torque from a large spinning shaft
would have on the structural elements of the building.
Similarly, experts in factory productivity were those who
could organize the individual work cells to align with the
spinning shaft. These professionals, and many more, had
an implicit pact with the status quo and no one of them
had enough scope or incentive to change things.

Brian Arthur didn't elaborate, but my suspicion is that
the eventual change did not take place because the
established firms finally saw the light (although a few
probably did). My guess is that newer firms emerged
without the predisposition to steam engines and spinning
shafts, ultimately displacing their more established
competitors by being nimbler and more efficient. This is
exactly what we are seeing now with the "digital native
companies." Companies that are less than 15 years old,
typically did not invest heavily in what we now consider
to be "legacy" systems, and as such have less inertia to
overcome.

Most established companies will gradually be displaced
by their nimbler, digital native upstarts. This book is for

the handful of companies who will choose to change
rather than be displaced. We now know that it is
possible, and incredibly productive, to profoundly
change the way enterprises approach information
systems implementation. It is a relatively simple change
– but that doesn't mean it will be easy.

A handful of firms has already embraced this digital
revolution and are enjoying the benefits. An amazingly
large percentage of established firms, though, continue to
double down on approaches that make things worse.

This book is for those who wish to reverse their death
spiral.

This is not a technology. This will not be a one-time
project. This is a movement. You must commit to the
movement and steer your firm toward this new set of
behaviors and priorities. Unfortunately, it is far easier to
buy some new technology than it is to commit to a
lasting change in approach.

THIS MOVEMENT REQUIRES EXECUTIVE SPONSORSHIP

We've been working on helping clients affect this
transformation for almost twenty years. At first, we
focused our efforts on mastering the latest and greatest
technologies. However, we have gradually come to
appreciate that the real problem surrounds business and
culture, and the solutions will have to be implemented by
executives. At its core, this movement is about changing

deeply held beliefs about how information systems should be justified and built.

This volume is for the business executives who wish to lead this charge. We have two more volumes queued up to help the designers and implementers, but without executive sponsorship, there won't be anything to design or implement.

In each of the case studies we describe in this book, and in all our experience with client projects, it is clear that there won't be a "quick fix" to the disintegration of information and the high cost of changing information systems that has been brought on by the application-centric approach. There are small and incremental projects that can be done along the way. The change is not very expensive, and once it gets going, is self-funding (the savings from eliminating wasteful IT spending in early projects will provide ample financial runway).

IF YOU ARE NOT AN EXECUTIVE

There's a chance you may have picked up this book without being an executive, and that's fine. You may very well gain some valuable insights, and learn about some important things that go on "behind the scenes" of data management. However, do recognize that if you don't change the context within which you are working, you will not get any closer to the transformation. Learning how to design a Data-Centric system while you remain stuck in an application-centric enterprise will make very little net difference.

Our advice to the modelers and technologists who are reading this: find and adopt an executive patron. Improving your own game isn't enough – you need to help change *the* game. Most potential sponsors won't be helpful; executives who have figured out how to succeed in the business side of a large enterprise have adapted to thrive in the status quo. It will take some intuition to determine who is up for changing the game. Until you find this person, you will be frustrated.

Some technological movements (like the push toward agile) can gain traction with purely grassroots efforts (i.e., without top management endorsement). However, the move to a Data-Centric approach is different. If you don't have senior management endorsement for this transition, you might as well give up.

Despite all the challenges to innovation, here are three bits of good news:

1. **Inflated project budgets provide working capital for change.**

As we saw in <u>Software Wasteland</u>,[3] the average cost of implementing systems has grown so bloated that it creates cover for doing the right thing. A typical

---

[3] Software Wasteland, How the Application-Centric Mindset is Hobbling our Enterprises, Dave McComb https://amzn.to/2IpssKd.

enterprise systems implementation project (say a new payroll system for a $ billion company) can easily cost $100 million. The contingency budget for such a system is typically 20% (which by the way history has proven to be woefully short). A Data-Centric alternative can often be proposed for a fraction of the contingency budget (not just a fraction of the project budget).

2. The costs to begin implementing changes are small enough to remain under the radar.

Sometimes, despite your best efforts to explain and justify your ideas, management just won't get behind a new initiative because it is so abstract. Some of the ideas in this book fall into that category. A non-executive sponsor may choose to build some part of a Data-Centric architecture in a skunkworks[4] to prove, and to make more tangible, the potential improvement. Keep in mind, though, that no matter how cool the proof of concept, if it doesn't become part of the mainstream development process, it doesn't matter.

3. Exotic technology can fund doing the right thing.

---

[4] The term "skunkworks" refers to a project that is sanctioned by management, but is intentionally kept separate to prevent the established culture from causing the project to regress to the status quo. The term came from the Lockheed P-80 Shooting Star project in World War II. The Shooting Star was the Air Force's first jet fighter and was conceived and built in 143 days. Lockheed housed the project in a tent in a parking lot in Burbank that was near a plastics factory. The smell from the factory gave the project the name "skunk works."

IT is a business of trends; different technologies come in and out of fashion more rapidly now than ever. It is possible to "fad surf" these technology waves in a way that is beneficial to the firm. Instead of merely using the most recent fad as a resume-padding exercise, it is possible to create a work plan in which new technology contributes to long-range improvement.

These three points give us hope for change. Current application-centric projects are so expensive that they leave room in their contingency budgets to experiment with novel approaches. Portions of the Data-Centric architecture can be built out without gathering a great deal of attention, and new technology fads can often be leveraged to begin the movement to Data-Centric technology.

If you're not sure where to start in looking for funding, consider some of the current major IT fads. It's often easier to get funding for current technology, and this can be leveraged to start your Data-Centric journey. At the time of this volume's publication, a few examples of major IT trends include:

1. **Cloud.** Most firms are moving to the cloud now in one way or another. Those who merely do a "lift and shift" (that is, take their current architecture and re-implement it in the cloud) may see a modest reduction in operational spend, but those who use the opportunity to rethink their entire

application deployment approach may reap huge benefits.

2. **Machine Learning**. Almost every large organization today runs multiple machine learning projects. Many have discovered that rationalizing and understanding their data assets provides huge benefits to the machine learning (as well as other) projects.

3. **Knowledge Graphs**. Most of the digital native firms (certainly Google, Facebook, Netflix, and Twitter) have Knowledge Graphs at the core of their architectures. For the firms that wish to emulate this and create their own enterprise Knowledge Graph, the Data-Centric approach is a rapid way to get there.

4. **Digital Transformation**. Over the last several decades, line of business executives mostly ceded control of their key information systems to the IT department, who often further ceded them to outsourcing contractors. The move toward "digital transformation" was originally centered on making the customer experience more seamless. What this movement is doing is giving line of business executives permission to retake control of key information systems. If your company has a digital transformation initiative already underway, you can leverage the initiatives we discuss in this book. If you do not

yet have a digital transformation initiative, this is an excellent time to start one.

This book aims to inspire confidence in the viability of the Data-Centric approach. Executive sponsors must be convinced to "stay the course" over the relatively long time this transformation will take. To this end, we will describe some tools you can use to make your case:

- Existence proof – presenting several case studies of firms who have done this already.

- Logical proof – laying out the argument based on the component parts of the solution.

- Existential need – revisiting the conclusion from Software Wasteland that we can no longer afford the status quo.

- Vision – creating a clearer future state to aspire to.

- Historical analogy – exploring similar historical transitions.

- Procedural help – providing step-by-step instruction on how to get from here to there.

All of this and more will be discussed within this first volume of our Data-Centric trilogy. First, though, we have a bit of housekeeping to deal with: what exactly are we talking about with this idea of "Data-Centric" software development?

CHAPTER SUMMARY

It is no longer feasible to continue implementing enterprise information systems in the dis-economic application-centric fashion we have been doing for decades. The alternative, the Data-Centric approach, which we will detail in the next chapter, does not require exotic new or expensive technology. It can take advantage of new technology trends, but is not dependent on them. It requires discipline and constancy.

CHAPTER 2
What is Data-Centric?

Our position is:

> A Data-Centric enterprise is one where all application
> functionality is based on a single, simple, extensible
> data model.

First, let's make sure we distinguish this from the status
quo, which we can describe as an *application-centric*
mindset. Very few large enterprises have a single data
model. They have one data model per application, and
they have thousands of applications (including those
they bought and those they built). These models are not
simple. In every case we examined, application data
models are at least 10 times more complex than they
need to be, and the sum total of all application data

models is at least 100-1000 times more complex than necessary.

Our measure of complexity is the sum total of all the items in the schema that developers and users must learn in order to master a system. In relational technology, this would be the number of relations (tables) plus the number of all attributes (columns). In object-oriented systems, it is the number of classes plus the number of attributes. In an XML or json based system, it is the number of unique elements and/or keys.

The number of items in the schema directly drives the number of lines of application code that must be written and tested. It also drives the complexity for the end user, as each item, eventually surfaces in forms or reports and the user must master what these mean and how they relate to each other to use the system.

Very few organizations have applications based on an extensible model. Most data models are very rigid. This is why we call them "structured data." We define the structure, typically in a conceptual model, and then convert that structure to a logical model and finally a physical (database-specific) model. All code is written to the model. As a result, extending the model is a big deal. You go back to the conceptual model, make the change, and then do a bunch of impact analysis to figure out how much code must change.

An extensible model, by contrast is one that is designed and implemented such that changes can be added to the model even while the application is in use. Later in this book and especially in the two companion books we go into a lot more detail on the techniques that need to be in place to make this possible.

The Data-Centric world is concerned with data models that emphasize what the data means (that is, the semantics). It is only secondarily, and sometimes locally, about the structure, constraints, and validation to be performed on the data.

Many people think that a model of meaning is "merely" a conceptual model that must be translated into a "logical" model, and finally into a "physical" model, before it can be implemented. Many people think a conceptual model lacks the requisite detail and/or fidelity to support implementation. What we have found over the last decade of implementing these systems is that done well, the semantic (conceptual) data model can be put directly into production. And that it contains all the requisite detail to support the business requirements.

And let's be clear, being Data-Centric is a matter of degree. It is not binary. A firm is Data-Centric to the extent (or to the percentage) its application landscape adheres to this goal.

DATA-CENTRIC VS. DATA-DRIVEN

Many firms are (or, for some, they at least claim to be) "data-driven." This is not quite the same thing as Data-

Centric. "Data-driven" refers more to the value or weight of data in decision processes. A non-data-driven company relies on human judgement as the justification for decisions. A data-driven company relies on evidence from data.

Although they are different, data-driven is not the opposite of Data-Centric. In fact, they are quite compatible. However, merely being data-driven does not ensure that you are Data-Centric. You could drive all your decisions from datasets and still have thousands of non-integrated datasets.

Our position is that data-driven is a valid aspiration, though data-driven does not imply Data-Centric. Data-driven approaches would benefit greatly from becoming Data-Centric. The simplicity and ease of integration makes data-driven efforts easier and more effective.

WE NEED OUR APPLICATIONS TO BE EPHEMERAL

The first corollary to the Data-Centric position is that applications are ephemeral, and data is the important and enduring asset. Again, this is the opposite of the current status quo. In traditional development, every time you implement a new application, you convert the data to the new applications representation. These application systems are very large capital projects. This causes people to think of them like more traditional capital projects (factories, office buildings, and the like).

When you invest $100 Million in a new ERP or CRM system, you are not inclined to think of it as throwaway. But you should. Well, really you shouldn't be spending that kind of money on application systems, but given that you already have, it is time to reframe this as sunk cost.

One of the ways application systems have become entrenched is through the application's relation to the data it manages. The application becomes the gatekeeper to the data. The data is a second-class citizen, and the application is the main thing. In Data-Centric approaches, the data is permanent and enduring, and applications can come and go.

DATA-CENTRIC APPROACHES ARE DESIGNED WITH DATA SHARING IN MIND

The second corollary to the Data-Centric position is default sharing. The default position for application-centric systems is to assume local self-sufficiency. Most relational database systems base their integrity management on having required foreign key constraints. That is, an ordering system requires that all orders be from valid customers. The way they manage this is to have a local table of valid customers. This is not sharing information. This is local hoarding, made possible by copying customer data from somewhere else. And this copying process is an ongoing systems integration tax. If they were really sharing information, they would just refer to the customers as they existed in another system. Some API-based systems get part of the way there, but there is still tight coupling between the ordering system and the customer system that is hosting the API. This is an improvement but hardly the end game.

As we will see later in this book, it is now possible to have a single instantiation of each of your key data types—not a "golden source" that is copied and restructured to the various application consumers, but a single copy that can be used in place.

THE DATA-CENTRIC VISION

The central idea of a Data-Centric enterprise is the existence of a single, simple, extensible data model. Let's examine this a bit deeper.

> Everything should be made as simple as possible, but not simpler.[5]
>
> Albert Einstein

We have observed that most enterprises have at their core a conceptual model that consists of a few hundred

---

[5] This is Roger Sessions "simplification" of Einstein's original "It can scarcely be denied that the supreme goal of all theory is to make the irreducible basic elements as simple and as few as possible without having to surrender the adequate representation of a single datum of experience." From "On the Method of Theoretical Physics," the Herbert Spencer Lecture, Oxford, June 10, 1933.

concepts. By concepts we mean the sum total of the classes (e.g., tables and entitles) plus the properties (e.g., columns and attributes). These are the distinctions with which programmers work. Because they are displayed in forms and reports, they are also the distinctions with which end users must deal.

Let's put this in contrast to what is typically implemented in a large enterprise. Very few applications have models that are simple. A typical application has thousands of concepts. Some Enterprise Resource Planning systems (ERPs), such as SAP or Oracle's ERPs, have hundreds of thousands of concepts, as do Electronic Medical Record systems (EMRs). Individual systems are already many orders of magnitude more complex than what is needed to manage the entire enterprise. When you combine many of these complex systems together, the sum total is staggeringly complex. We thought we hit a high-water mark when we discovered a firm that had 100 million concepts in their implemented systems, but the early results from another firm predict that they may hit the 1 billion mark. This is 1 billion concepts, not 1 billion records—obviously, they have many billions or trillions of records. But the fact that they have come up with 1 billion ways to type or categorize such records indicates just how far we have come from the ideal.

We were at a client recently, and Jans Aasman made an observation that was so profound, it is still ringing in my ears. Jans is CEO of Franz Inc.,[6] the provider of a leading semantic graph database. Jans has had a front row seat and participated in many projects that ushered in the exact kind of change we're referring to in this book. He said, and I may be paraphrasing a bit:

> *I was at a prospect firm recently, in the healthcare space. One of their analysts told me in a rather matter of fact way that they had data on patients in over 4,000 tables in their various systems. This is the end result of forty years of relational thinking: it didn't occur to them that this was wrong. This arrangement essentially guarantees that you will never have a unified view of your patient.*
>
> Jans Aasman

We outline in this book how to reverse this. One of the key enablers is simplicity.

It is easy to come up with simple models. People do it all the time. However, usually when people oversimplify, the complexity goes somewhere else. Usually that somewhere else is in application code. Another important resting place for complexity is manual procedures. It is possible (and is actually the norm) to construct procedural workarounds to handle the cases not handled by a system. People often build rule-based systems on top of other systems to handle some of the distinctions omitted from the system.

---

[6] http://www.franz.com.

It is possible to make a data model overly complex. It is possible to over simplify it. Is there a goldilocks zone where the model has "just the right" amount of complexity? We are finding that there is such a zone. We are finding it to be far smaller than even we would have thought when we started on this journey over a decade ago. There are techniques, which we will get to later, to keep a lot of the fine-grained distinctions from polluting the design space of your core model.

We have been finding that optimal levels of complexity are in the many hundreds of concepts, 300-500 seeming to be a reasonable target.

The interesting thing from the perspective of human cognition is that there is a real difference between 10,000 concepts and 400 concepts. It takes years, maybe an entire career, to really master 10,000 concepts. But 400 concepts are within reach of most motivated participants. As one of our clients said recently: "This is at a level that a motivated analyst could internalize it over a weekend." This is especially true when half of those 400 concepts are very well known and already understood and agreed upon (including the concepts of "Person," "Unit of Measure," and "Geographic Location").

We usually start with a model of an enterprise that consists of a few hundred concepts. Next we focus on a particular subdomain (see extensibility below) for a given application. Our unstated goal is to add fewer than 25%

new concepts for each subdomain. What that does is recognize that the sub-domain is literally a subdomain and not something entirely new.

> An ontology is a conceptual model that captures formal definitions of classes and properties. A formal definition is a machine process-able set of rules that can be used to infer such things as class membership or the existence of property assertions.

In one case, we built a first cut enterprise ontology (a core conceptual model of the firm), which consisted of about 400 concepts. This was a company that made electrical devices. We created a sub-domain model for their product catalog, specification, and configuration management. We then converted the data from their existing product catalog to the product ontology. When we went back and reviewed what we had done we noticed that their existing catalog management system (just one of hundreds or thousands of systems they had) had 700 tables and 7000 attributes, or 7,700 concepts in total. The part of their new model that we populated with the data from this system consisted of 46 classes and 36 properties (later in the book we will get to how these kinds of models can have fewer properties than classes, which is literally impossible in traditional systems). The fascinating thing was that as we began building product selection and configuration management systems on this new model, we proved that the new model had not dropped any of the fidelity of the original model. We had

all the distinctions with about 1% of the complexity:
((46+36)/(700+7000).

This is important at two levels:

1. Everything you do with this model (write code
    against it, write rules in it, use it for big data
    analytics) is simpler, cheaper, and more reliable.

2. It shifts dealing with the data from the province
    of the expert (the person who understands the
    7,700 concepts and how they relate to each other)
    to the true owners and consumers of the data.

EVOLVE-ABLE

"Extensible" in the definition really plays out two ways:
evolvable and specialize-able.

A system is evolvable if it can gracefully adapt. Stuart
Brand wrote a charming book called How Buildings
Learn,[7] in which he made an observation and built a
conceptual model. The observation was that some
buildings gracefully change as new tenants adapt the
building for new purposes. And some buildings don't
evolve well. He adopted a model called "pace layering"
to explain this.

---

[7] How Buildings Learn, Stuart Brand 1995 https://amzn.to/2vaudlR.

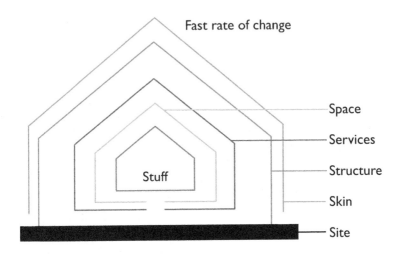

A building is a set of "shells" that want to change at different rates. The "structure" (bearing wall and the like) might change every 100 years if at all, while "services" (plumbing, air conditioning, etc.) change every 30-50 years, "space" (interior non load bearing walls might change every 15-25 years, and "stuff" (furniture) is changing all the time. If the architecture of the building allows them to change independent of each other, the building can evolve.

A well-crafted Data-Centric architecture has these same properties. The foundation of a Data-Centric architecture is what Marshall Cline and Mike Girou called "Enduring Business Themes." [8] There are core concepts in enterprises that remain stable over decades or longer. If we base our model on these, we have stability. If we layer

---

[8] Enduring Business Themes, Marshall Cline, Mike Girou
https://bit.ly/2V7Dwlp.

on the things that change more rapidly over time, and allow them to change without disrupting the core, we can evolve in place.

SPECIALIZE-ABLE

Specialize-ability is the other side of the extensibility coin. Not only do we want the model to evolve over time to keep pace with overall demands, we would like it to be locally different.

With traditional approaches, if one department needs some extra features in an application system, they generally have two choices:

1. They can convince the rest of the firm to accept the changes to incorporate the features, or

2. Build their own system.

Historically there hasn't been a good way to share most of the data and most of the functionality. Object-oriented design was meant to accomplish this, but in practice it wasn't flexible enough.

Going back to our inventory control example: imagine that one department decided they wanted to store perishable items; produce, for instance. They would like to extend the model to include "good until" dates and perhaps base their cycle counting on this information. But they don't want to re-implement all the ordering, stock keeping, issuing, and receiving functionality.

A system that will allow them to do this is specialize-able. All the core functionality should still work with the produce. We should be able to value all the inventory, regardless.

SINGLE BUT FEDERATED

Recall our definition of Data-Centric:

> A Data-Centric enterprise is one where all application functionality is based on a single, simple, extensible data model.

This doesn't mean that there is only one data model. It means that the data models within a firm are derivative from one, which we often refer to as the "core model." Being a derivative from an extensible core means that detailed concepts, described in domain sub-models are defined in a way that knowledge of the core concepts, provides a general sense for the meaning in the sub-domain.

Having a single model does not imply having a single database. In most installations there will be many databases that conform to the core model. The architecture to support Data-Centric will ensure that these databases can be reached in a federated manner. That is, that one query can reach into multiple aligned databases and provide a combined result.

The single-core model provides a vocabulary to execute queries. To the extent that the specialized models are derivative from the core, then a query using the core vocabulary will pick up the specializations. Again, to our inventory example, if we query for inventory, we will get widgets as well as watermelons, even if we didn't know ahead of time what a watermelon was. We will get the "good until date" of the watermelon, even if we didn't ask for it.

There is a second aspect to the implementation of the Data-Centric approach, which is the ability to federate a query over many repositories or databases. Traditional relational databases have been tuned in such a way that it is very difficult to execute a single query across more than one database. One of the key aspects of a Data-Centric architecture is its support of federated queries. We will go into this in more detail in <u>The Data-centric Architecture</u>. Briefly, a federated query is one where you write one query, and it is distributed to multiple databases, each of which solves a portion of the problem, and then the results are recombined.

These federated queries can include databases that were loaded directly into the Data-Centric model, as well as existing legacy databases that have been mapped to the Data-Centric model.

ENTERPRISE APP STORE

The Data-Centric approach makes possible an "enterprise app store." Anyone who has enjoyed the app store (which is to say everyone) might well wonder: "why can't I have this for my enterprise?" The double-barreled short answer is integration and functionality. That is, the end consumer app store "works" because of the low bar on data integration. For the most part there is very little integration between apps, as they are mostly unaware of each other. What little integration exists is done by the user. You might load your contacts into an app, you might build an "IFTTT" (IF This Then That) app to synch up some of your data, but really this is a personal ad hoc bit of integration and not enterprise integration. And the functionality in the app store is pretty lightweight.

You can't really manage inventory, process orders, settle trades, underwrite insurance, adjudicate claims, or any of the many other complex functions that an enterprise routinely performs on a lightweight app store type app.

Despite this, we believe the application ecosystem of the future will look and act a lot more like the AppStore of today, but there will be two major changes

The first is that in the enterprise app store all the apps will be built from the shared data model. Everything the app knows will come from the data model, and the result of everything the app does will be returned to the shared model. You might have an app that does inventory cycle counting. What it knows about inventory, location, quantity on hand and recent transactions, it gets from the shared model and the data bound to the shared model. The app supplies some algorithms, perhaps to suggest how often to count which items, or maybe one that suggests counting when the system thinks the item is out of stock. This is both the easiest time to count (either there are zero or you find a few) and it is the time to count when it will make the most difference (the difference between having 11 or 12 items on hand doesn't make a lot of difference, but if you discover you have one item on hand when you thought you had zero, you can continue to sell the item).

The important thing is that the results of the count (that it was taken, who took it, what the count was, as well as any adjustments in quantity on hand if there were any) are put back in the shared data, using the shared concepts, in a way that any other application can take advantage of them.

This is a huge difference. It means that if you find or build a better cycle count app, you can just start using it. No data conversion. No other apps that must change. With current technology, usually if you want better cycle counting you end up implementing another giant monolithic application.

The other advantage is not every department has to use the same cycle counting app. Maybe the department with large outdoor inventory wants their counts optimized around travel time. This environment means that everyone doesn't have to use the exact same application, they merely have to conform to the same model and the same rules.

The other thing that will be different between the enterprise app store and the current consumer app store is the economics.

When the app store was launched, many veterans scoffed at the idea of 99 cent applications. It is now an $80 Billion industry.

The enterprise app store apps will not be 99 cents. In most cases they will have to be bespoke built to the enterprises core model. So the universe of buyers will not be large enough for anyone to make money at 99 cents.

But we expect that most enterprise app store apps, will be a few pages of code and could be built in a few days. You might have them built by your in-house agile teams, or an industry of firms that are good at making apps and aligning them to your model may spring up. Most enterprises will need several thousand of these apps. If they cost $1,000 each (which is what I think the market would like settle in to) you would have all the application functionality of your firm built for a few million dollars.

More importantly any one of them could be swapped out for $1,000 or so.

We believe that the end game of the Data-Centric approach will be a viable market for low-cost small-scale bits of functionality, coordinated through a shared model.

INCLUDES ALL TYPES OF DATA

The Data-Centric approach provides an approach to one of the most vexing problems in the enterprise information system space, that of integrating structured and unstructured data. As of 2019, the following types of data exist: :

- *Structured data*—data in relational databases.

- *Semi-structured data*—data in XML, json, html, or other structures that are not rigid tabular structures but have some structural clues.

- *Network-structured data*—social media and other data expressed in graphs.

- *Unstructured data*—documents, notes, memos, and even audio / video.

For the longest time, integrating these types of data was the holy grail: an imaginary ambitious thing that would probably never happen. It is now routinely doable. In chapters 8 and 9 we will explore the standards that support bringing various types of data into a single representation. For now, be aware that the integration of structured, semi-structured, and unstructured data is a solved problem.

THE ECONOMICS OF THE END GAME

Right now, in large enterprises (in the private sector or government), the cost to get a major system implemented is in the tens to hundreds of millions of dollars. The cost of keeping all the implemented systems stitched together is even greater.

I'm going to ask you to imagine an end state that may sound a bit utopian at the moment, but I will flesh out the details in this and the companion books. In this end state, you have a single core model for all the concepts shared across your enterprise. As we suggested earlier, the model consists of 400 concepts that everyone at your firm understands and agrees with.

The model is extended into a dozen subdomains that cover in more detail each of the more specific and specialized areas of your business. Each extension adds dozens of more specialized concepts and a host of fine-grained "taxonomic" distinctions.

> Taxonomy: Taxonomies are ways of organizing or structuring information. They are often thought of as being hierarchical, but our experience suggests that there are many useful taxonomies that are flat. The more important distinction for our purposes is that taxonomies have few complex or custom relationships.

Concepts in your core model (e.g., "customer," "purchase order," or "treatment plan,") have many complex relationships to other concepts. The taxonomic distinctions to use to further refine the characterization of your concepts (e.g., "VIP," "domestic," or "chronic") are simple tags. They have few, if any, relations to each other and can be treated as stand-alone tags used to categorize other things.

There is a library of shared functional routines that provides IT functions in the application-specific data model and programming language that, traditionally, are coded over and over again to satisfy the common function. These shared functions do things like:

- Layout fields on a screen

- Detect the change to a data field

- Forward a message, such as an email, in response to a stimulus

- Provide mathematical functions, such as net present value and internal rate of return

- Compute geospatial, such as area or distance between two points.

This library is finite in size. Depending on your industry and requirements, it might be as small as a few hundred functions. Each of these functions is tied to concepts in your core model. For instance, the geospatial functions are tied to place-related concepts. These functions are coded and deployed in a way that is language and operating system independent.

There exists an environment for bringing data and functions together declaratively, that is, there is little need for new code.

In this world, we will have forgotten why we even needed the monolithic application. As we contemplate the need for new functionality or new data structures, we will just add them. My observation is that the impetus for most new application projects is that there is a small number of functional deficits with the current systems, and these deficits are deemed to be too hard to implement in the existing system.

In this new world, the new requirements will be added to the ecosystem incrementally. We will cease thinking of application projects.

The economics of this are staggering. High-risk, multi-million-dollar applications will be replaced with small incremental improvements. Integration projects, which require small armies to maintain, will be replaced with information that holds its own integration.

CHAPTER SUMMARY

A whole new world is unfolding for sponsors of enterprise information systems. By flipping the prevailing paradigm on its head, we can see how enterprise information could be differently harvested, organized, and consumed.

This change is not a technological change. It is a change about how we choose to organize, describe, and deploy information systems. This new way of envisioning systems puts data at the center. Applications (think app store-sized applications) will come and go. They will conform to the data structure that exists rather than imposing their own. Everything they do will be reduced to data and be self-describable, and in such a way that if the application were to vanish tomorrow, the data would be sufficient to carry on.

This arrangement has many fortuitous benefits, one of which is the ability to not only integrate all the structured data that exists in a firm, but also to take this to the semi-structured and unstructured data of the firm.

This is the vision. What comes next is how to get there and some examples of firms that have already achieved it.

CHAPTER 3
Getting There

The preceding vision is clearly not the status quo in most firms. The rest of this book and its companion volumes will go into more detail, but let's outline what is needed to get from here to there.

WHAT IT REQUIRES

Moving a firm from its application-centric habits to a new Data-Centric paradigm will require changing a lot of things simultaneously. Everything is arrayed against the change agent.

> *After living with their dysfunctional behavior for so many years (a sunk cost if ever there was one), people*

*become invested in defending their dysfunctions
rather than changing them.*[9]

Marshall Goldsmith, Mojo

The resistance to changing to this new way will be both subtle and diffuse and, at the same time, pointed and specific.

This will require someone (or preferably a group of someone's) who can understand and finesse the kind of resistance that an undertaking of this type will require. There will be overt and covert resistance, as well as pure inertia.

INERTIAL RESISTANCE

The inertial resistance is perhaps the trickiest. It isn't intentional. It isn't aimed at you. It isn't even aware. In a large organization, executives have internalized a way of getting things done. It involves the particular seasonality of budgets. It concerns whose agendas need to be reinforced. There are norms around how projects gain momentum. In some organizations, the most successful gambits involve positioning one's project to be the answer to regulatory issues. In others, the case needs to be made that a given system is a "burning platform" and must be abandoned as soon as possible. Others have the luxury of long-term plans to tie one's initiatives to.

---

[9] https://bit.ly/2XpIpDO.

Whatever the prime movers, most executives have worked out how to get projects on the docket and get them approved, perhaps without even being consciously aware of the strategies they are employing.

In addition to considerations around getting projects considered and approved, there are norms around project sizes and how much pre-work must be done to justify a project of the "normal" size. We worked with a State Agency that was funded on a biennial (every two years) basis. There were never funds assured for any project for more than two years in duration. That organization had learned, over decades, to scope projects to be a bit less than 24 months in duration, and to have interim deliverables such that they didn't get to the end of the biennium and have nothing to show. A two-year project (typically with dozens of developers) demands a bit of planning: typically, at least a three-month feasibility study and a six-month requirements study. If everything goes well, the project is found to be feasible, and the requirements suggest a project scope that fits with the trial balloon budget numbers floated before the project scope had been nailed down.

There is nothing wrong with any of this. Indeed, this is a learned response to a set of goals and constraints unique to each organization. I bring this up because what you will be attempting to do will not fit this pattern. Therefore, it will be hard to find allies, because no one has any history with doing things this way. They may well agree with you and not know how to move forward.

OVERT AND COVERT RESISTANCE

I just covered the resistance of people who may actually want to do what you are intending to do. Let's talk about those who don't want this type of endeavor to succeed.

Enterprise IT is almost a $4 Trillion a year industry, growing at a healthy rate. There are tens of thousands of firms who are invested in continuing the growth trajectory they have been on for the last several decades. I met a Systems Integrator senior business development VP who was in the midst of closing in on an $800 Million CRM project. He had been working on this account for years. Do you think he was interested in how they could take 99% of the cost out of this project? (Spoiler alert: he wasn't.) Had I been motivated, I'm sure I could have figured out how to take 10% out of the cost and risk of the project, and it's something someone with an $800 million project would be interested in. But I'm not interested in perpetuating this madness.

On the other side, the buyer's side, there are equally interesting incentives and habits to overcome. An executive will have been working on a major project for years. He or she will have compared notes with executives in other similar sized organizations and functions. After you have spent $5 million on a requirements project, which reinforced your preconceived belief that your new project was going to cost $120 Million (+/- a laughably precise $15 Million delivered by very earnest consultants whose confidence springs from the reams of spreadsheets backing up their conclusion), you would be hard pressed to launch an implementation project for $2 Million.

Furthermore, you have managers who have hundreds to thousands of direct reports, and very large budgets who are not motivated to think about drastically reducing the size and importance of their empires. You will find a sponsor of a rival project (as we did) who just committed $20 Million to a packaged application who are not interested in being embarrassed by a pilot project that shows that a better result could have been (was) delivered at a fraction the price. We are aware of another firm who built an incredible customer support system, using what we would describe here as a Data-Centric approach (although they didn't call it that at the time). It was implemented at a major customer, and delivered unprecedented metrics, such as issue resolution on first call, call prevention, reduced number of agent handoffs, and reduced churn. And yet the project was cancelled. There were other executives who were betting on an alternative approach who, while they had inferior technology and methodology, had superior political skills, and carried the day.

I don't say this to generate despair. I say this to reinforce my earlier point: this endeavor will require an executive who is senior enough to deal with these issues and, at the same time, junior enough to have the time and the inclination to take on a long-term change project of this type.

That is a lot of bad news. However, interestingly, there are a lot of things this change doesn't require.

What It Doesn't Require

First and foremost, this doesn't require a large budget. Every case where we have seen this succeed, it has done so with a modest budget (6-12 full-time equivalents, typically at the core of the change process, and then a similar sized team for each conversion or initiative).

It does not involve exotic or proprietary technology. It can be, and has been, done with clever adaption of traditional technology, as we will see in the first set of case studies. If you choose to leverage Semantic Technology (which we make a case for later in the book), you will be pleased to find that once you get over the initial unfamiliarity hurdle, there is a wide array of tools and platforms built on a set of open standards in a way that enables true interoperability. You will find many open source alternatives for many parts of your architecture, and for those where you prefer the comfort of commercial support, their adherence to open standards prevents vendor lock in.

It does not involve extremely rare expertise. Every year there seems to be a new bidding war going on for the must-have expertise da jour. Currently, it is machine learning and artificial intelligence. The last few years it was data scientists. Next year it will be something else. When these fads hit, the cost for talent can rise considerably. You will need some talent, just not those that everyone else is looking for. One of the two talents you will need will be the ability to model well at the conceptual level. These skills are findable, and the companion book, Data-centric Pattern Language, will help someone who is well-versed in conceptual modeling come up to speed on the additional skills they will need to model in this environment. Likewise, for the foreseeable future, there will not be suitable fully formed platforms available to purchase, and you will likely have to staff a team to build out your architecture. The other talent you will need will be solid technical architects and developers who are fluent in modern languages, such as JavaScript and python or java. The other companion book, Data-centric Architecture, will flesh out the additional considerations they will need to incorporate.

THIS IS A PROGRAM, NOT A PROJECT

A project has an individual and specific goal. Achieving that goal is the completion of the project. Building a dam is a project. Assuring flood control, non-fossil fuel energy, or adequate sources of agricultural water is a program. A program has goals, but these goals evolve over time, and the goals require many interrelated projects to contribute to its success. A program may decide to change the sequence or type of projects it employs to achieve its ends. But it is still possible to tell whether a program is succeeding or not.

Decades of IT implementation have caused us to focus on projects. Each project is individually justified and executed. It is rare that they are seen as contributing (or detracting) from a larger scale program. That's what is different about the Data-Centric movement. The Data-centric movement involves many projects, but it is a program. The success of the program rests on the degree to which the firm's application functionality is based on a single, simple, extensible data model. As that overall program goal is achieved, many other metric-based goals will improve as well (e.g., cost to implement new functionality, percent of budget spent on integration, and IT spending as a portion of revenue).

THE TRANSITION TO A DATA-CENTRIC APPROACH REQUIRES DISCIPLINE AND CONSISTENCY

Organizing around programs rather than projects allows for shifting priorities. Successful completion of individual projects is not the key predictor of success. Yes, you will be running several projects, and most of them need to be at least partially successful, but this isn't the main thing. You may be encouraging others to start projects, and their contribution to the program is more important than their own specific success.

You will launch projects that are only tangentially related to the program's long-term goals. You may launch a project that is primarily about getting more skills in the organization. You may launch a project that makes the program more visible to the enterprise. Many of the early projects will have an immediate application payoff coupled with a contribution to the architecture.

A few early wins will provide the cover needed to deliver a few projects that are necessary but may not be as publicly defensible.

THE IT FASHION INDUSTRY

What you will notice if you look through the long-term lens is that IT is a fashion industry just as much as the garment industry. We read trade magazines and go to conferences in order to find out what approaches and technologies are "trending." Developers have learned that padding one's resume with the latest languages and frameworks is the golden ticket to higher wages. Knowing the acronyms is key. Even pronouncing them correctly is important.

While executives are not expected to be technically up to date, they need to understand which technologies apply to their business and are expected to be making strategic bets in those areas. As I am writing this book, virtually every company in North America has a blockchain project in progress. 90% of them are expected to be abandoned[10].

Gartner has made a mini-industry tracking where each emerging technology is on its inevitable trajectory. Gartner calls this trajectory the "hype cycle."

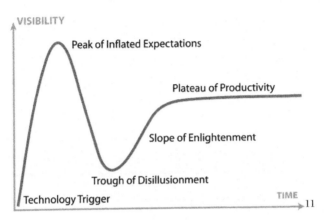

Most people who have been in IT for a while recognize the pattern. In phase one a new technique or product is invented. The early adopters understand the technology and especially understand how the technology can contribute to real benefits. At this point, it is no different from diffusion of innovation as seen in other technologies.

IT technology differs just after we get through the early adopters. As a new technology begins to show promise and benefit, the hyping starts to kick in. Hype in the IT

[10] https://bit.ly/2ymjapZ and https://bit.ly/2x9FXpM.

[11] https://bit.ly/2Pi6xp8 (marked as available for reuse).

world is a many-headed beast. Developers jump on
bandwagons, sometimes just out of curiosity or novelty.

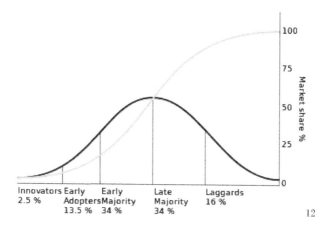

12

Many developers are intelligent and curious and are
drawn to new developments. They also are often
handicapping technologies and trying to guess which
ones will most enhance their future earning power. When
a hyped technology goes mainstream, companies end up
in a bidding war for the talent to implement it. Because
these technologies are new, it is often hard to evaluate
competency directly, and employers tend to rely on
proxy measures, such as experience reported on a
resume.

Adding fuel to the hype cycle fire are IT vendors who
either promote the new IT technology directly or attach
it to their current offering. Right now, for instance, all
products are cloud enabled.

12 https://bit.ly/1PhwzDX.

As news of the early successes begins to surface, executives are increasingly drawn in. It is a combination of fear of missing out and perceived competitive necessity, worrying, "if our competitors get a head start on us here, we might not be able to catch them."

Once a technology begins to get hot, these three forces (developers padding their resumes, vendors pushing new technology and fear of missing out) combine to overheat it very rapidly. The "hype" (vendor marketing which is often over promising the potential outcome) combined with demand (developers and business people, each with their own motives) combine to create a rush to the technology. This corresponds to the peak of Gartner's hype cycle.

Unfortunately, most of the people rushing in to fill the demand are not up to the task. Additionally, many of the projects meant to leverage the new technology were not well thought out as executives and developers rushed to apply the technology. This creates what Gartner calls the "trough of disillusion." At this point, most of the people who adopted the new technology are disappointed because "this stuff doesn't work." Thus, the technology falls out of favor.

However, in most cases, the technology had legitimate value. After all the failures wash out, the few projects that had the right talent and target show the way forward. After some notable post-trough successes, executives feel safe in re-approaching the technology.

Luckily by this time, the hype has come and gone. At this point, it is easier to find truly experienced developers, and the race for talent isn't as severe.

IS THE DATA-CENTRIC APPROACH A FAD?

By this point, you may be wondering whether this whole new Data-Centric approach might just be another passing fad. So far , it isn't exhibiting those characteristics. There are no products hyping their "Data-Centric-ness," nor are there developers leading with their Data-Centric street cred.

Could it become a fad? It is possible, and we want to stay on the alert for signs that it is happening, but I doubt it will. In my opinion, it will not be technology as much as mindset and discipline that prevent Data-Centric methods from becoming trendy.

As far as I know, "agile" never went through a hype cycle, and yet it has arrived. A great deal of development now is agile. Again, I think this is more because agile methods weren't associated with a specific technology, but were more about a change in the way of doing things.

CAN DATA-CENTRIC METHODS BENEFIT FROM OTHER FADS?

Can we or should we "fad surf" for the benefit of our Data-Centric initiative? It may seem cynical or opportunistic, but I think we should. Initiatives like the transition to Data-Centric methods are hard to fund. The progress is quite gradual. Fads, on the other hand, are very easy to fund. If you time it right, your firm will be demanding whatever new technology that has suddenly become "it" in your industry.

Attaching your Data-Centric initiative to an emerging fad can be a win/win. You will gain funding and senior executives' attention by becoming part of the flavor of the month that the enterprise is getting behind. The other side of the win (which we will pick up in the chapter "Data-Centric and Other Emerging Technology") is that almost all the past, current, and upcoming IT fads that we are aware of actually benefit from a dose of data-centrism.

Fad surfing brings the danger of losing focus. This is tricky. The main thing becoming Data-Centric requires is consistency. A spacecraft on a mission to a distant planet can often get there faster by diverting and flying to another planet in a way that is designed to increase its speed through the "slingshot effect."

You want to get a slingshot effect from your close encounters with technology fads without falling into their orbit. If you find yourself caught up in the hype of the fad, you will end up off course on your primary objective.

FROM FAD SURFING TO NEW DISCIPLINE

Enterprises have a great deal of inertia around their information system implementation practices. While the fads of the technology industry can provide a nudge toward change, and can often free up budget for change, as has been demonstrated time and again, new technologies don't in and of themselves create lasting change.

Lasting change comes from changing the way things are done. Our observation is the needed changes are in two main areas:

- New Modeling Discipline
- New Delivery Architecture

NEW MODELING DISCIPLINE

We have trained a generation of data modelers how to build silos. Those thousands of data models you have in your enterprise were each independently designed. In some cases, by competent designers and modelers. But there has been no discipline and no impetus for these designs to converge into a single data model as we suggest here. This will require discipline and a change in the modeling approach.

For an idea of the types of changes that will be needed in modeling, we can examine the undisciplined state of the art in data modeling as it is currently practiced.

If you work for a large enterprise, you have repeatedly built or bought applications that cover many of the same concepts. If you look at the data models behind these systems, you will be amazed at the ingenuity. You will be gobsmacked when you find out how many different ways there are to model the same thing. This overlap in concepts, and lack of overlap in implementation is exactly why systems integration is hard. If every application structured their common data the same and named all the same attributes the same, systems integration would be just a matter of copy and paste. But it isn't. It isn't even close.

Let's examine where this variety comes from.

There is a great deal of methodology and mathematics around structuring a data model once you decide what you are modeling. This includes the practice referred to as normalization. Normalization is a step-by-step process to move from a poorly organized first cut of a domain design to one that optimizes its arrangement. If two modelers using the normalization process started from a similar, even flawed, starting point, they should end up with the same result.

The issue is that two modelers covering the same domain do not start from the same starting point.

It is worth examining briefly now, and in more detail in the companion volume, why two modelers will create wildly different starting models.

The first thing is that almost all data modelers start with a "clean sheet of paper." That is, they go into a design session ready to model whatever they encounter. They interview subject matter experts who describe the data that they work within their own terms. Data modelers jot down these terms and begin experimenting with ways to organize it.

While they start with a clean sheet of paper, whatever they capture first has a profound impact on how the design occurs. From that starting point there are many more design choices. Almost any aspect of a model can be done at various levels of abstraction. Many aspects can be parameterized or intentionally made more flexible. At this point, all the terms are made up and gain their own sort of permanence.

The endpoint of this process is what gives us such rich variation just where we don't want rich variation. And keep in mind, the model for a packaged application is based on a core set of interviews that were conducted, decades ago, usually, and often in industries and settings far removed from yours.

This is a discipline, and it will not come naturally or easily, but if we are going to have a Data-Centric enterprise, we are going to need to change the way we build our data models.

NEW DELIVERY ARCHITECTURE

And we are going to need a new delivery architecture.

One reason this sounds daunting is that for most projects, we just accept the delivery architecture of our application packages. Really, it's the average delivery architecture of the application packages we're implementing now.

In the early 90s, most enterprises were writing "fat clients" (Visual Basic, Power Builder or their equivalents) with most of the application logic in programs installed on PC clients. They talked pretty directly to relational databases. In the late 90s, the stack mostly moved to server-based systems, mostly based on Java, still with relational databases. Most firms experimented with message-based architectures and/or API-driven architectures. These days, RESTful endpoints and JavaScript frontends are mostly the norm.

When I say that we will need a new delivery architecture, that sounds like a big ask. And yet, we have been continually changing our delivery architecture for as long as we have been implementing systems. The only thing that may be a bit scary is that we have mostly accepted architectures from packaged applications as the starting point or prototype architecture, and then extended from there. In the Data-Centric world, we are not going to have applications that are setting the norms for architecture because we are not going to have applications as we currently think of them.

As we suggested earlier and will elaborate more fully in the third part of this trilogy, this architecture will have very little application code. There will be small "applets" comparable to applications in the app store or Google Play, but there will not be monolithic applications as we know them.

Along the way, the new architecture must co-exist with existing systems. This is essential. New functionality in the Data-Centric architecture is going to be adding on to what is there more than replacing what exists. As your architecture matures, you may find point solutions where you can replace legacy functionality with the new more flexible type. But there will be such a long period of co-existence that one of the key aspects of the architecture will be how it will promote this easy integration.

Luckily, this is one of the strengths of this architecture. For right now, we are just going to state that standards and tools exist to make it easy for traditional systems and Data-Centric systems to interoperate. We will go into some of the specifics in the chapter on formal semantics.

As you bring functionality to the shared enterprise model, there will be code that performs some standard functionality in a more general fashion. The chapter on "model-driven everything" will explain how this works and what the scope will be. Some functionality that was traditional in the realm of the monolithic application, such as security, identity management, constraint management, and notification, will move from application logic to the architecture.

CHAPTER SUMMARY

This is not going to be easy. There is no "quick win."

The good news is this entire program will cost less than an average application package implementation. It will deliver incremental improvements along the way and, once the program gets into gear, will pay for itself as it goes.

But the changes are quite profound. It will change the way people think about design. It will change the architecture they use to implement systems. It will change the way systems are funded. Initially, you will have very few co-conspirators. You will be forced to adapt to whatever IT fad is being funded in order to fund continuous improvement. It will take a long time. By the time it becomes the new normal, there will be many who are willing to take credit for it.

But this is the nature of profound change. It's not for everyone.

CHAPTER 4
Why We Need This Now

We've outlined a better future. We've described why the status quo is arrayed against you. These dynamics have been true for a while. Why is now the time to act?

There are two main contributors to the timing:

1. The status quo is getting exponentially worse.

2. The alternative is finally gaining momentum.

THE STATUS QUO IS GETTING EXPONENTIALLY WORSE

As we saw in <u>Software Wasteland</u>, the current status quo regarding enterprise software implementation is a disaster. Typical project timelines and costs are routinely

10 times what modest best practices would suggest[13]. In the previous volume, we suggested some measures that would curb the worst of these excesses. This volume picks up where the other left off. Curbing the worst excesses is a step in the right direction, but what we want to do is take what we have learned and take it to the next level.

This book is about what next-generation enterprise software is going to look like. We explore it from first principles as well as some of the pioneers who have already established a beachhead in this brave new world.

First, let's do a recap of what is really causing the problem so that we can juxtapose it with a new way of building systems.

CODE CREATES MAINTENANCE

One thing we know with a great deal of certainty is the more code you have, the larger your maintenance burden. Some of this is the "latent defect rate." We know that all software has latent bugs. These are flaws that haven't yet manifested themselves because the right combination of circumstances has not happened. But they are there, lurking. Very sophisticated quality software development and testing can reduce the extent of latent defects, but nothing eliminates them.

---

[13] Software Wasteland has several examples of this as well as the Standish Group https://bit.ly/2xaHNH7.

In <u>Code Complete</u>, [14] Steve McConnell reports that the industry average defect rate is between 15 and 50 per KLOC (thousands of lines of source code). These "latent defects" manifest themselves when you least desire them. You have no choice but to staff up to handle this. Your 10 million lines of code system, therefore, has at least 150,000 latent defects.

Some "cleanroom" development environments have managed to get the latent defect rate of code as low as 3 per KLOC (a great reduction from 15-50), but this takes Herculean effort. It is far easier to reduce the defect rate by reducing the number of lines of code you are dealing with. When you drop the amount of code by half, the latent defect rate drops by half. It's pretty easy to drop the amount of code in half and to do it over and over again. Indeed, we have done some projections that suggest that it is not unreasonable to suggest that the number of lines of code a large enterprise needs to support could drop by 100 to 1000-fold.

Further, even without the out-and-out failures that the latent defects usually germinate into, is the impact of change in the environment. Every change to regulation or business strategy, even changing computer operating systems, puts a strain on the code base. The larger the code base, the more likely there are hidden dependencies and the larger the strain.

---

[14] Code Complete: A Practical Handbook of Software Construction, Second Edition 2nd Edition. by Steve McConnell https://amzn.to/2PizgKs.

A related issue is: whose problem is all this excessive code bloat? Certainly, the code that a firm has written or had written for it is their problem. Even any acquired software that has been modified.

What isn't as obvious is that code you don't even have direct access to has complexity roughly proportional to the size of the code base, which you eventually end up shouldering. If you use a DBMS (Database Management System) or ERP (Enterprise Resource Planning) that consists of hundreds of millions of lines of code, there is a very good chance this complexity is keeping you locked in, and that any slight change or desire to migrate will be hindered by the complexity of the code base.

Given that many large firms are dealing with billions of lines of code, they are teeming with diseconomy. Each new project makes the situation worse.

Perversely, many implementers brag about the number of lines of code they are bringing to bear or are creating for the solution, as if this were a good thing. The much-maligned Healthcare.gov implementation project at one point boasted of the 500 million lines of code that were involved in its implementation. It is as if a manufacturing firm were bragging about the amount of their toxic waste, as if this were a measure of productivity.

The main takeaway: application code is the problem. Strive to reduce it as much as you can.

COMPLEXITY CREATES HIGH PRIESTS

Complexity, as we will use the term here, refers to the number and difference of interacting parts, and the variety of their interactions. In software systems complexity mostly manifests as lines of code, and most complex application systems became that way through complex database schemas.

My observation is that most people have a comfort zone around complexity. As they begin solving a problem, they bring in more data, more considerations, more factors, more structure, more tables, and more data in general. The solution gets a bit more involved and more nuanced.

New information is grafted onto initial structures. Often this creates additional complexity. Seasoned developers recognize they are doing this and set aside periodic development tasks to "refactor" and restructure their solution, based on new information that would have changed how they organize things had it come in a different sequence.

Whether the problem solver periodically refactors their solution or not, the solution gradually becomes more complex. Because this happens gradually, the solution architect has time to internalize and consolidate the complexity in their mind.

Everyone else has not had the same amount of time to absorb this complexity. This creates a monopoly of understanding in the mind of the creator, or often someone who has devoted a great deal of time to the solution. These experts, while helpful in the short run if you're trying to interface with the solution, are actually part of the problem.

By running all requests through these "high priests," we further entrench silos and complexity.

APPLICATION-CENTRICITY CREATES SILOS

Executives rail against "silos," yet not a great deal of time is spent on understanding where silos come from, or how to prevent them. As a result, it is easy to rail against them even as you are re-implementing them.

We have silos because of our application-centric mindset. Every time we say, "Let's not reinvent the wheel," or, "Buy before build," we commit ourselves to instantiating another application database. It will inevitably have copies of some other datasets (if it is an ordering system, it will no doubt have customer and product data), but this borrowed data has been converted, restructured, and renamed to conform to the application being implemented.

When we are finished, and when we have finally converted some of our old data to the new format and added new data, we will have successfully created yet another silo of data.

Very few projects recognize the full scope of the integration debt that implementing a new application system involves.

SILOS CREATE THE NEED FOR INTEGRATION

Between 40-70% of most IT budgets are spent on integration of some fashion. Logically speaking none of this is necessary. "Systems Integration" seems like a value-added endeavor, but it is only because of what made it necessary.

Imagine a world where cars were built for $20,000, but it took $40,000 worth of rework to make the car drivable. If non-drivable $20,000 cars are all there is, then the "car rework" industry is a high value-adding industry. Once someone figures out that the cars could have been made correctly in the first place, it becomes obvious that the rework was only value-added because of the faulty build process. Rework, as the quality movement in manufacturing has so succinctly pointed out, is waste.

This is where we stand with enterprise systems. Systems Integration is rework. Information silos create the need for integration.

Whether built in-house or acquired, the end result of decades of software implementation is a landscape of silos, expensive to attempt to integrate after the fact.

LEGACY CREATES ENTRENCHMENT

Everyone laments their "legacy" systems. For example, what is it about a payroll system implemented 20 years ago for $2 million that would make it cost $20 or $40 million to replace now (and at great risk)?

Keep in mind your legacy system was built with what we could now consider the equivalent of stone tools. We worked with a major Forest Products company that had a payroll system that had been written in Assembler Language on punched cards. Many of our State Agency clients have legacy systems written in languages like COBOL and Natural, which are not known for their developer productivity.

So why was it so much cheaper to build the original system than its replacement? Some people say that it is because the requirements are so much more complex now. I have built and implemented several payroll systems in my career, and I continue to be apprised of developments in the area by virtue of being, among other things, the chief payroll officer for our consulting firm. In my opinion, payroll has become about 10% more complex than it was 40 years ago. We have always had to calculate gross pay based on a set of rules that included which hours had been worked and which of them had to be considered overtime (and therefore be eligible for time and a half or double time). Payroll systems have always had to be aware of holidays and had to accrue and charge vacation hours. Payroll systems have always had to deal with a wide variety of pre-tax and post-tax deductions. We have always had to garnish wages for various reasons. Deductions have always been based on percentages and fixed amounts and often had annual caps. We have always had tax codes that varied based on marital status and deductions, and every state has always had their own tax tables, forms, and reporting periods.

As near as I can tell, a payroll system these days has a few more types of deductions and the states and federal government now allow online automated payment, which is a big plus. We often now add on some functionality for benefits management or skills management, but the core functionality of a payroll system is scarcely greater than that which was implemented in punched cards at a Forest Products company many decades ago.

One of the reasons that a payroll system implemented decades ago was so much easier and cheaper, despite the lack of good tools, was when the original system was built, there was almost nothing for it to be connected to, and nothing that depended on it.

Once the system is in place, other systems begin to rely on it, in subtle and overt ways. A downstream system builds a feed, and someone else takes extracts for their system; others use the identifiers from the first system and become dependent on them.

In a mature environment, replacing a legacy system is akin to performing a heart transplant: getting the old heart out and the new heart in is relatively straightforward, hooking up all the arteries, veins, getting nerves reconnected and keeping the patient alive throughout the process is where the work is.

INFLEXIBILITY CREATES SHADOW IT

"Shadow IT," "Satellite systems," "Rogue systems," "Dark IT," and even many "End User Computing" solutions refer to the smaller departmental solutions that grow up around your enterprise systems.

These systems further exacerbate the silo and legacy problems described above. Typically, each has a feed from the larger system (often an undocumented feed), which is one of the key contributors to keeping legacy systems in place—nobody knows how many of these systems are being fed from a corporate system and what would be impacted if it were replaced (and if the API changed).

The typical shadow IT system is built in Microsoft Access or Excel. It is remarkable how many mission-critical systems have one or more Excel spreadsheets in their data provisioning pipelines. There are several instances of firms using detailed Sarbanes Oxley Analyses to prove the provenance of the numbers in their financial statements. Many of these firms, to their surprise, found that their data had been processed through a series of spreadsheets.

What should cause alarm is the fact that 85% to 90% of spreadsheets have serious flaws. The error rate is 1% to 5% per cell.[15] [16] [17]

Why do people build and maintain shadow IT systems? The primary reason is the inflexibility of the corporate system. Gartner estimates that 35% of information system spending goes to shadow IT.[18] In our observation, four of the most common reasons people build shadow IT systems are:

1. To categorize or classify information in some way that is not supported by the corporate system.
2. To add additional data attributes to a data record in a corporate system.
3. To combine data from more than one source.
4. To perform analytics – often relatively simple calculations appropriate for a spreadsheet.

All four of these are symptoms of a deeper problem: the corporate systems are too hard to change and are monolithic. If the corporate system were easy to change, these categories and additional data and analytics could

---

[15] https://bit.ly/2IGPqvL.

[16] https://on.mktw.net/2mnS9xE.

[17] https://bit.ly/1tsAoub.

[18] https://bit.ly/2KTx25E.

have just been applied in place. Consider the waste in copying a set of corporate data to a local data store, adding a category, and performing some simple analysis. As a one-off, this isn't a punishing bit of overhead, but once this becomes a regular job, the API must be supported, the download job must be scheduled, the satellite system must be maintained, and the results typically aren't available to the source system because they have no place to store them.

Another perverse side effect of this state of affairs is the number and variety of these satellite system ossifies the legacy system. The stewards of the legacy system don't know how many feeds are dependent on their data structures, and even the smallest change could have dire, unpredictable downstream consequences. Legacy maintenance grinds to a standstill.

The related problem is that corporate IT systems are just that: corporate. It is the same system for everyone. There is typically no mechanism for departments to share a system and yet have their own customization. In this book, we will describe how a Data-Centric view promotes this and allows us to have variety in the context of standardization.

MEGA PROJECTS CREATE MEGA FAILURES

Large information systems continue to have embarrassingly high failure rates. The 2014 Standish

Chaos report reported a rate of 41% failure and 55% "challenged."[19] To save a bit of math, that leaves only 4% "successful."

While the overall success rate has been at this level for some time, there is more bad news in the Standish data: the bigger the project, the higher the failure rate. As our world and its data landscape grow increasingly complex, big projects are becoming the norm.

There is a silver lining to the observation that most large IT projects fail: Failed projects don't make your overall information architecture worse than it was. However, most "successful" projects do. In the world of application-centric, every new successful project introduces another mostly redundant data model and dataset, and thereby increases the cost of systems integration.

As we will see in the next section, the key driver to enterprise information system cost is complexity.

WHERE APPLICATION COMPLEXITY COMES FROM

Application software is complicated. It is among the most complex artifact ever produced by humans. A great deal of the complexity comes from the fact that every single line of code is different, and any line of code, when executing in a running application, may have adverse

---

[19] https://bit.ly/2GvkVr5.

outcomes on other software. Even a simple application is complex, and most enterprise applications are not simple. Many have millions of lines of code. Changes to this code are fraught with risk.

The deeper question is, "where did the need for millions of lines of application code come from?"

Function Point Analysis is a tool for estimating the size of an application software project. The Function Point Users Group[20] have been refining this approach for over three decades. The approach relies on counting the number of components (inputs, outputs, and the like) and the complexity of each. The chart on the facing page from Software Metrics[21] summarizes the key part of the estimating methodology.

These factors are used to estimate how complex a software project will be. If you drill down, each of the factors eventually bottoms out into schema complexity. The number of "External Inputs" is the number of classes or tables or transactions that are being inputted, which is one type of schema. The evaluation of low, average, or high complexity is based on the number of elements per each input (and is therefore also driven by the complexity of the schema). Each of the other five components is equally 100% driven by the schema complexity. Adjustment factors, such as the complexity

---

[20] http://www.ifpug.org/.

[21] https://bit.ly/1OTdLv2.

of the organization or the technical environment, are applied after the total number of points has been established.

Type of Component	Complexity of Components			
	Low	Average	High	Total
External Inputs	__ x 3 = __	__ x 4 = __	__ x 6 = __	
External Outputs	__ x 4 = __	__ x 5 = __	__ x 7 = __	
External Inquiries	__ x 3 = __	__ x 4 = __	__ x 6 = __	
Internal Logical Files	__ x 7 = __	__ x 10 = __	__ x 15 = __	
External Interface Files	__ x 5 = __	__ x 7 = __	__ x 10 = __	
Total Number of Unadjusted Function Points				
Multiple Value Adjustment Factor				
Total Adjusted Function Points				

It follows if you double the complexity of your schema, the number of function points will double, and the complexity and effort of your entire application will double. (The adjustment factor is a constant, so whether you are adding 25% or 125%, the end result is the project doubles in size).

What isn't obvious from this methodology is how easy it is to double the size of the schema on an application project, and therefore double the size and complexity of the resulting system. Indeed, the mega projects are just several doublings of complexity, most of which are unnecessary. To get an idea of how easy it is to let complexity run rampant, what follows are a few case studies in complexity.

A CASE EXAMPLE IN COMPLEXITY

We worked with a firm that had hundreds of "products" (their product was data and so they referred to datasets or Application Programming Interfaces (APIs) as "products"). Most of these products had thousands of attributes. Occasionally they would try to migrate a customer from one of their products to another. This invariably led to trying to find someone who was an expert in the "from" product system and the "to" product system. It was very rare that they could find someone who was an expert in two systems. And anyone who was, was in such high demand it was hard to get his or her time.

Most product migrations were very difficult negotiations between two experts, who spent a great deal of time working out the similarities and differences of their data representations.

Ultimately, this firm produced an inventory of all the attributes they had in all their systems. There were 150,000 items in their inventory. This sheds a bit of light on how unnecessarily complex things can become.

Our core model for this firm had about 500 concepts in total. The stretch was that many of the distinctions in the 150,000 were not different attributes (60,000 of the 150,000 were address-related attributes) but were contextual. In a rich model, the context distinctions can be modeled in an economy of concepts. But mapping

150,000 attributes directly to their primitive representation would be time-consuming. What we did instead was create a faceted model that provided a way to group and distinguish the distinctions they had made in the 150,000 attributes and in the attributes in all their various products.

Implementing a set of systems with a collective schema of 150,000 attributes, when 500 would suffice, is not making the problem twice as complex as it needs to be, as I was suggesting above. It is making it 300 times as complex. To put it another way, they doubled the complexity 8 times. This is recounted to get a sense for the extent of the complexity that exists in many corporate environments and the opportunity for improvement, and to remind us that in the absence of determined effort to turn back complexity, it continues to creep.

SEPARATION AND ISOLATION

Part of the problem stems from the separation that has been encouraged by the way we build systems. As systems become more complex, there is a tendency to splinter them off into smaller, more manageable pieces. Once separated, they become isolated. This makes it easier to work on because you don't have to consider the impact on the rest of the firm, and therefore, each piece tends to develop on its own.

Designers and developers believe that the cost of coordinating and conforming are too high and prefer instead to isolate themselves and solve their own problems.

This natural tendency is one of the driving factors that lead to silo creation. This starts a vicious cycle. As the systems become more separated, the first thing they do is implement their own instance of a database. Very often, especially if the new application is a package, it will be not only a separate instance of a database, it will be a separate DBMS (Oracle versus Microsoft SQL versus IBM's DB2). Once the separation is in place, the models begin evolving on their own. There is nothing drawing them back together and everything allowing them to drift further.

Agile development has a concept they call "technical debt." It is the recognition that many short-term fixes erode the overall structure of the code built up to that point. They recognize if the quick fixes aren't addressed, the system will gradually take on the characteristics of a legacy system (expensive to make simple changes). They set aside periodic sprints to "refactor" their code, which essentially means restructure the code as if you knew at the beginning what you know now. There are many patterns that emerge after the fact that create easier-to-modify systems.

The analogy for systems of systems is "integration debt." Each point-to-point interface that you build adds to integration debt. When developers (or their managers) succumb to the attraction of isolation, they unknowingly introduce "integration debt." Like all debt, it must eventually be repaid.

HUMANS IN THE LOOP

The way we build and integrate systems requires a great deal of "human-in-the-loop" processing. Even within a single application, the act of "joining" data between two tables requires a human, with knowledge of the metadata, to write the queries that will "join" the tables.

The problem becomes far greater when there is more than one systems involved. Humans are in the loop to extract data from one system and post it to another, or to access the APIs of one system and then those of another.

The "human in the loop" factor doesn't drop to zero immediately when you begin your Data-Centric journey. As long as we use legacy systems, we will need humans to map them and more. However, we will gradually wean ourselves off a great deal of the non-value-adding portions of that work.

THE NEGATIVE NETWORK EFFECT

There is a vicious cycle in the middle of all of this. As firms invest more and more in more complex systems, the cost to introduce a new system raises the cost even more, and the integration costs spiral ever upward.

The rising integration costs cause developers to try to isolate themselves, which leads to further development of silos. The need to get something done fast leads to short cuts, which often delay taking on the kind of change that will improve things.

COMPLEXITY MATH AND THE WAY OUT OF THE QUAGMIRE

There are three factors that generate the complexity in a typical enterprise. They are multiplicative; any one of them doubles the complexity of the whole. Doubling two of them quadruples the complexity of the whole and doubling all three amplifies it by eight times.

The three factors are:

1. How many data models you have (which is essentially how many applications you have, as with very few exceptions, each of your applications has its own data model).

2. How many concepts there are in each data model (this is the number of tables + columns or classes + attributes) that application programmers must program to (there are often concepts that are managed by the architecture that the application programmers needn't be affected by).

3. The average number of lines of code per concept (how many lines of code, on average, are added to a program when the schema is increased).

What follows is a very conservative example for a typical billion $ company:

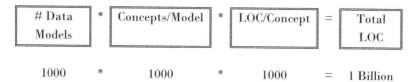

# Data Models	*	Concepts/Model	*	LOC/Concept	=	Total LOC
1000	*	1000	*	1000	=	1 Billion

1 Billion is a US billion (9 zeros and not a British Billion with 12 zeros). Each of these numbers is very conservative. Most of our clients have 3,000-15,000 applications. Few applications have under 1,000 concepts, and many purchased applications have 10,000 plus. QuickBooks, to use a well-documented example of a presumably well-written application, has 1,300 lines of code per concept.

I think a reasonable goal should be to drop each of these by a factor of ten. Strive to have 100 applications, each of which has, on average, 100 concepts they code to and use model-driven development to drop the LOC average to way under 100 per concept (for many use cases there will be zero lines of code, but the occasional bespoke app will bring the average up). We will discuss model-driven development later in the book, but for now take it to be an approach to delivering application functionality that does not rely on writing new code for every slight variation in application functionality.

This will result in 1 Million lines of code to manage, which is a fantastic 1000-fold reduction in complexity. That is a stretch goal. But if in pursuing this you "merely" dropped each in half (very doable), your overall complexity drops by a factor of 8 (or 88.5%).

CHAPTER SUMMARY

The complexity of our information systems is directly proportional to their cost, both to implement as well as to operate and change. Complexity is what drives the inflexibility of the typical application information system. The cost of our information system is directly proportional to its complexity.

We are so, so far from optimal that opportunity abounds. We can make great strides by reducing the number of applications we manage (rationalization) by reducing the complexity of the models in our systems (through elegant design) and by reducing the amount of code needed per concept (through model-driven development and other techniques). Reducing all three has a synergistic effect. This is the aim of this movement.

The superiority of the Data-Centric approach has been around for a long time.[22] Why is now the time to tackle this?

---

[22]Database Management: Objectives, System Functions & Administration, Gordon Everest https://amzn.to/2UQ9pzG.

CHAPTER 5
A Deeper Look at Data-Centric Approaches

In the second chapter, we briefly defined "Data-Centric," and outlined some of the benefits that come from transitioning to this approach. In this chapter, we're going to fill in a lot more of the specifics.

IT'S THE DATA, STUPID

The shift from putting applications in the center of our universe to putting data in the center is profound.

When you break it down, a computer application is data and behavior. With the application-centric mindset, we tended to focus on the behavior first. We tended to automate the manual processes that we had done prior to automation.

Analysts strung together sequences of tasks into "workflows." An inventory system might have tasks like these:

(EOQ is Economic Order Quantity, a calculation of how many units you should repurchase, based on things like cost, lead time, or recent demand history.)

Not shown in this simple workflow is that each step is actually a transformation of inputs into outputs. In a physical workflow, inputs might be components and outputs assemblies. In data workflows, inputs and outputs are data. We'll see that most tasks exist to turn inputs into outputs. In general:

We can apply this framework to a specific example from above:

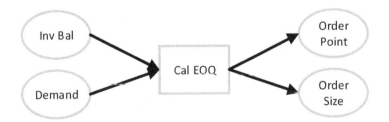

In this way, the process is defining what it needs the input data to look like and what the output data will look like (e.g., how it will be structured, how it will be labeled). Developers love this. They create "json" (JavaScript Object Notation) data structures that consist of name/value pairs and their problems are solved. Even relatively modern approaches, such as defining APIs, are usually thinly-disguised process automation.

TASK-CENTRIC IS A TRAP

Yet in most applications, the tasks are a means to an end, and not an end in themselves. In most applications, if we had the data (the answer) then, executing, the processes would be pointless. But by automating the process, we have hardened these localized data structures and the code that accesses it.

The alternative is to not allow processes to define data, and to not have processes have knowledge of each other:

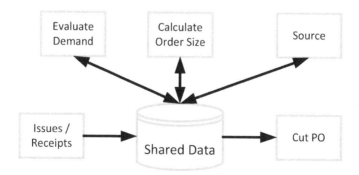

On the surface, and in a simplistic illustration like this, this looks like every application ever built on a database. At one level, it is. We must explore why database-based applications didn't solve the problem.

The main reason this didn't solve the problem is that the scope of sharing didn't match the problem to be solved.

An early attempt at solving this problem was to make the database in the middle big enough to handle all the functions of the firm. This was the birth of ERP (Enterprise Resource Planning) and other related "Integrated Applications." Because of the technology they were using, as the scope increased the complexity increased even faster.

At first it seemed like a tradeoff: you could either have one immensely complex integrated application or hundreds to thousands of simpler (but, unfortunately, not appropriately simple) systems. Try as they might, few firms achieved the singled integrated application nirvana. Most paid the price of the integrated application implementation and still had hundreds of satellite systems to handle functions the integrated application couldn't. This is the worst of both worlds.

If you have 100 applications, each with its own database, each application is sharing with 1% of the firm.

Even the small bit of sharing that goes on within an application is done at too high a cost. Reflect on the simple inventory system illustrated above. What if one of your departments is inventorying fresh produce (which has a short shelf life). As we said earlier, maybe you'd like to swap out the routine that calculates order size (maybe for these items you'd rather have smaller orders more frequently).

There are no commercially available applications that will allow this level of modularity and composition, and very few custom applications that have come close to this.

In <u>Software Wasteland</u>, we go into a great deal of detail why what we've been doing up to this point is making things worse. Very briefly, it is because all the knowledge of the structure of the data—its naming, validation, security, integrity, and even the meaning of the data—is locked up in the application code, which is the hardening of the manual processes that preceded it.

Rather than reiterate that, we need to concentrate here on the alternative.

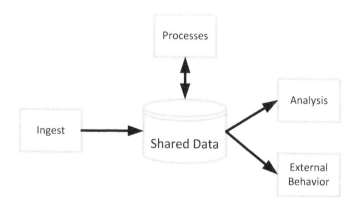

In the Data-Centric approach, the data comes first. Taking the Data-Centric approach to individual applications will provide significant benefit. But the real power comes from being Data-Centric at the enterprise level. We can imagine a time where whole industries will be Data-Centric, but we need more firms to be Data-Centric before industries will sign up for this.

The remainder of this book describes the Data-Centric approach applied at the enterprise level. The principles can be applied at the application level as well as the industry level, but we believe the current "sweet spot" to most effectively implement the method is at the enterprise level.

To become Data-Centric we have to adopt the position that data is the key asset in a firm. This data exists independent of any application. We allow applications to come and go. The results of application behavior are persisted back in the data, which does not require any specific application to interpret.

To achieve a Data-Centric enterprise, we need self-organizing, self-aware, resilient data.

IT'S THE STUPID DATA

Data, as it been traditionally used, is not self-organizing, self-aware or resilient. Data is thought of as being passive, and code is the active ingredient working on the data. Data is too dumb to "know itself" and too weak to defend itself.

> My veal cutlet came down to the counter to beat the [crap] out of my cup of coffee. Coffee was too weak to defend itself.[23]

In this book, we describe what it takes to make data smart, self-reliant, and strong enough to defend itself. (And not take crap from any applications.)

It's very trendy now to implement "data lakes." A "data lake" is an approach that leverages what has been learned in big data projects to deal with a firm's legacy data. In the chapter called "How Data-Centrism Plays Well with Emerging Technology" we will go into more detail about how Data-Centric approaches can save the data lake from itself. For now, just imagine your data lake: all the data from all your current applications, laid down, more or less raw and unedited.

You might think that this is a Data-Centric approach; there certainly is a lot of data in a central place. Let's take this notion a couple of steps further. Imagine you had a data lake and you chose to run your entire company on it (including inventory control, payroll, and all your other processes). Imagine you did this without traditional application systems. Further, imagine that anyone with access to the data lake is allowed to update

---

[23] Tom Waits "Nighthawks at the Diner".

the data in place. This would not end well. Planes would fall out of the sky.

The problem, as most firms have found, is that even using the data lake as an analytic platform is problematic. Using it as a primary source system would be extremely challenging, and it's important to understand why. This is because many key tenets of Data-Centric systems were not implemented in order to overcome these limitations of data lakes.

The difficulties in using a data lake as the primary data source include:

1. Understanding what the data means.

In a data lake, this task falls to the data scientist, who frequently supplies meaning after the fact and in a very *ad hoc* fashion. One rising trend right now is the implementation of "data catalogs," which represent a baby step toward universal organization and understanding of the meaning of the data in the data lake.

2. Protecting the data from unauthorized access and/or update.

Every organization has rules about who should and should not be able to see or update various kinds of data. The current generation of data lake mostly skirts this by being downstream of where the data was created or collected. A future system needs to deal with this in a systematic way.

3. Ensuring the integrity of the data.

For consumers of data to trust it, we need to ensure the data's quality, consistency, and integrity.

4. Assembling all the appropriate data to solve a task at hand.

In traditional relational systems, an analyst must understand a great deal of "metadata" (schemas, which describe where the data is stored and how it is structured) to write a query that can assemble data from more than one table. Similarly, with big data, or the traditional data lake, the analyst must know what all the keys in all the data structures mean in order to assemble datasets worthy of analyzing.

5. Packaging the data for human or external system consumption.

Finally, there needs to be a mechanism for packaging and presenting data, whether it be in forms, reports, or graphics.

Historically we have relied on applications to provide these functions for us locally, separately, and redundantly for each application. Providing this in a simple, Data-Centric fashion is a challenge, but as we will see, not impossible.

We will document some firms that have done this using traditional technology, then introduce some technologies (primarily Semantic Technology, graph databases, and model-driven development) that make this a far more tractable problem, and then follow with some case studies of companies who have used these technologies to implement Data-Centric systems.

Before we get to that, we are going to fill in some of the additional emergent properties that come from this approach.

THE "WHAT IF" VIEW ON DATA-CENTRIC METHODS

Imagine for a minute, that you made all your data accessible from one point, and that you addressed the five issues (understanding, protecting, ensuring integrity, assembling, and packaging) outlined above. What would this allow you to do?

- You could execute transactional updates against the equivalent of your data lake.

- By knowing a small handful of concepts, you could query all the knowledge and data of your firm, uncovering and learning additional distinctions as needed.

- Combine structured and unstructured data in a single query.

- Build enterprise level applications functional in days instead of months or years.

- Rather than continuing to spend most of your IT budget on integration, you would achieve integrated data with nearly no effort.

There are many emergent properties that come from this approach, including the following.

INFORMATION DISCOVERED IN USE

In a traditional system, you must know all the metadata before you can ask for information. You must know the names of the tables and the columns in order to request data from them.

With this new approach, you can query for a higher-level concept that you know and retrieve more specific versions of it you may not have known, and it may be attached to properties and data that you did not have prior knowledge of, but which you can easily infer or lookup. This is a concept that has been called, "follow your nose." With effective implementations, it is possible to begin by querying for known concepts and thereby following the links that are uncovered, you can discover, in context, far more about your data.

END OF DATA CONVERSIONS

In the current paradigm, every time you implement a new system, a big part of the project is "data conversion." Those who have experienced them know that the data conversion part of an application implementation project is a big and complex undertaking. This is because the data in the old system is named, structured, and managed to one data model. The same data has to be restructured, renamed, and often "cleaned up" in order to be ported to the new system.

This is not really value-added work. It is only necessary because you are moving between two arbitrarily modeled data structures. In the Data-Centric world, we will still incur a one-time conversion to get from the legacy data structure to the shared data structure, but this will be the last time a conversion will be necessary. New applications will conform to the structure, and the data will stay where it is, expressed and structured as it is. You may add to it, but you will no longer be converting it. There will be cases where you convert the structure for performance or analytic purposes, but this will not involve changing the application code.

With this next generation of systems, the application code (what little there is) is not based on the structure of the data but on the meaning. The meaning of business data changes much more slowly than its structure and representation.

FEWER MODELS

Right now, large firms have thousands of application systems. Each of which has its own data model. Smaller firms still have hundreds. Even tiny firms have dozens, without knowing it. There is a data model behind quick books (with 152 tables, 6958 columns; sales force has over 600 tables and more than 6000 columns). Even though a small business owner may not have to program these models, they still must deal with them. They must know which form to fill out, what the fields mean, and how to get from one representation in one system to a different representation in another.

By the way, any mid-level manager with a credit card can commit the firm to an amazing amount of integration debt without realizing it, by implementing a SaaS (Software as a Service) project. In fact, they will be quite proud of the improvements they have made, even while incurring this integration debt.

The first thing the Data-Centric movement offers is fewer models. Ultimately, we aim for one, federated model, which means one core plus a few dozen extensions. But, any movement in the direction of thousands to even hundreds or dozens is dropping complexity at laudable rates.

SIMPLER MODELS

The original promise of an ERP system (which originally was shorthand for integrating manufacturing with finance and HR) and EMR (which was originally to be the integration of all patient information in the healthcare industry) was to get to fewer models. This was a laudable aim. However, when the few models became hideously complex, this was found to be a Faustian deal.

It turns out that the ultimate competitive advantage comes from having the simplest model that covers all the requisite variety. What is weird is that we have found that individual applications can have their complexity dropped by an order of magnitude (tenfold / 90% reduction) relatively routinely. A "system of systems" that is the complex ecosystem of the typical enterprise can drop in complexity by 2-3 orders of magnitude.

INTEGRATION ALMOST FOR FREE

As you move toward a Data-Centric mindset, you will find that integration becomes less necessary. Consequently, the cost of integration drastically falls. Later in this book we'll explore in more detail why and how this happens. For now, a basic overview will suffice.

There are two levels of integration in a traditional system: within an application and across applications. Within an application, integration of data between tables is executed with queries. These queries rely on the fact that data in database systems has identifiers or "keys." However, the problem with the keys is that they are only locally unique. Very locally unique. There is only a guarantee that the key is unique in one database, in one table, and in one column. Because of this, an analyst must supply all the contextual data in the query to allow "joining" two tables together. This requires a great deal of a priori knowledge of the schema/metadata to get anything accomplished.

Integrating data between systems is even worse. As bad as the human-in-the-loop "join" problem is, within a single database, it is exponentially worse when you cross database boundaries. In the first place, you don't even have the option of a "join" and must do something far worse. Additionally, it requires detailed knowledge of the schema/metadata of two systems—two systems that are arbitrarily different. Many of these systems are complex enough that it requires people to dedicate a chunk of their career to the system to master its complexity. As a result, it can be quite difficult to find one individual with deep enough mastery of two systems to effect an integration. Instead, two experts are brought together to discover and negotiate an integration. This is largely why systems integration is difficult, costly, and brittle.

In the Data-Centric approach, as we will be detailing it here, integration is far simpler both within a domain and across domains, as it uses the same approach, but it is not reliant on mastering a complex schema.

In the Data-Centric approach, all identifiers (all keys) are globally unique. The identifiers are constructed in such a way that the contextual clues of database, table, and column are not needed to uniquely identify anything. Because of this, the system integrates information for you. Everything relating to an entity is already connected to that entity.

Writing queries becomes not an exercise in assembling information—it is already assembled—rather, it becomes a pruning exercise. This is the much simpler exercise of saying what subset of the connected information you are interested in and which parts you are not interested in. Remember the analyst who had patient data in 4,000 tables? To get a complete picture of a patient, someone would have to write a 4,000 table join. To the best of my knowledge no one has ever done anything quite that extreme. Most people find steeply diminishing returns after about a dozen, and query optimizers seem to give up long before this point.

In the kinds of systems we're describing here, the patients data would already be combined, waiting for you to prune away the bits you're not interested in at the moment.

MORE FLEXIBILITY

We will cover this in more detail later, but the Data-Centric approach grants freedom from predefined data structures, which means that the structures it does have are more open and can easily be extended or specialized.

When you build your system around tables or even the structures in an object-oriented system, you immediately buy into inflexibility. The next row in your table cannot have attributes that haven't already been defined for the rest of the rows in the table. The next object instantiated from your object-oriented class cannot suddenly have different attributes.

But, that is exactly what we require and propose for next-generation systems. The system will have a sanctioned way to flexibly add to existing structures, without completely abandoning the predictability of schema.

CHAPTER SUMMARY

In this chapter, we peeled the onion a bit more to describe, mostly through metaphor and analogy, what Data-Centric really is and how it differs from its predecessor. We declare that it is like a data lake with enough organization and architecture in place that it could be a source system, and at the same time provide the basis for integrated querying.

In addition to a high-level look at how a Data-Centric approach achieves this, we filled in a bit on the implications. We also described how the Data-Centric approach leads to fewer and simpler data models, less application code, nearly-free integration, the end of data conversions, and a flexible structure.

Before we get to others who have achieved this and more specifics on how this works, we want to spend a bit more time to get you thinking about what you will have to overcome to get this in place. For almost all organizations, this is a pretty radical departure from business as usual; as such, it cannot be taken up lightly.

CHAPTER 6
A Paradigm Shift

The Data-Centric revolution is disruptive, but not disruptive in the Clayton Christiansen[24] sense. When Clayton Christiansen coined the term, he was referring very specifically to innovations that served an un-met or under-met market segment with a product that was inferior to that being offered to the primary market segment, at a much lower price. Without crossover, these products would merely have created a new lower end submarket. What made some products disruptive, was their ability to continuously improve and eventually move up in the market from the underserved segments into the broader market. They are disruptive because of the effect they have on the incumbents in the industry.

---

[24] Innovators Dilemma, Clayton M. Christensen https://amzn.to/2UJj7DV.

Data-centrism may eventually be disruptive in the Clayton Christiansen sense, but that will be a secondary effect. It may well disrupt the Systems Integration and Application Package industry, but not by offering an inferior product to an underserved market. It may do this by changing the nature of the application implementation market. But before it does this, it needs to disrupt something more local: the internal application implementation and support infrastructure.

You can't just show up waving a big "Data-Centric" flag and expect people to adopt it right away. You must anticipate some resistance and plan appropriate responses. Earlier we chalked up such rollout problems as "politics." This was not untrue, but it was simplified. Now that we understand more about the nuances of a Data-Centric method, we can dig a bit deeper, and really try to understand these dynamics. When you anticipate the reasons why a company refuses to budge, you can handcraft strategies to work around their sticking points.

PARADIGM SHIFT

The term "Paradigm Shift" was coined by Thomas Kuhn[25] to refer to those times in history where progress was marked not by accumulating new information but by changing the way we think about the information we

---

[25] The Structure of Scientific Revolutions, Thomas Kuhn
https://amzn.to/2UttmXV.

have. Kuhn details many examples showing how hard it can be to prompt a major shift in an established discipline. In an established discipline, the thought leaders are already organized around and familiar with the prevailing way of doing things. Data that would suggest the need to adopt the new thought patterns is interpreted through the filter of the established order and often dismissed.

> *An important scientific innovation rarely makes its way rapidly winning over and converting its opponents; it rarely happens that Saul becomes Paul. What does happen is that its opponents gradually die out and that the growing generation is familiarized with the idea from the beginning.*[26]

Max Planck

Adopting a Data-Centric approach means making a paradigm shift, and that's no trivial matter. The barrier to change is not technical but mental; it's about how we think about our systems. In this chapter, we're going to discuss how paradigm shifts really occur, and the subtle nature of the resistance you are likely to encounter.

THE ORIGINAL PARADIGM SHIFT

Until about 500 years ago, the sun revolved around the earth. Or so it seemed. Such was the received wisdom. It

---

[26] The Philosophy of Physics, 1936.

seemed obvious. You could see the sun come up in the east, travel at a pretty constant rate across the sky and set in the west. And so did the fixed stars. And so, mostly, did the planets.

Initial observation of the planets revealed that they were "wanderers." They didn't stay in their positions relative to the fixed stars. They weren't darting around like shooting stars, but by carefully observing over the course of weeks you would see them move through the heavens relative to the stars.

Even closer and more detailed observation revealed something even more puzzling. Most of the time the planets moved in relatively straight lines. They occasionally observed what has been called "retrograde motion."

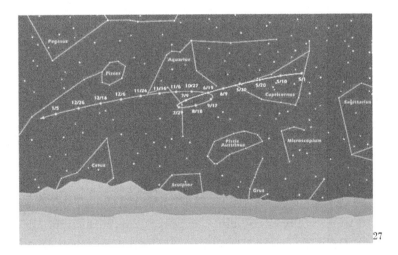
[27]

---

[27] https://bit.ly/2PizmSk.

For several weeks, a planet will move through the heavens. For most of the month of May, it wanders in the constellation Capricorn. By summer it is in Aquarius. It is about to leave Aquarius when it reverses course and starts heading back toward Capricorn. By the end of September is has reversed direction again. It leaves Aquarius in November and is in Pieces by December.

Astronomers of the day created more and more elaborate models and explanations for these anomalies. As each round of detailed measurements came in, the explanations became more tortured. It is a testament to how firmly we cling to our preconceived notions, that these models became more and more unlikely.

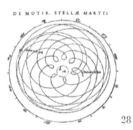

28

With hindsight it seems that once the problem was reconceived everyone would see the elegance and rush to embrace the new viewpoint. Nicholas Copernicus informally published his initial thinking on a heliocentric universe in 1514.

He labored for 20 years on the proofs and further implications of the theory and had most of his book <u>On</u>

---

28 https://bit.ly/2GqBC5O.

the Revolutions of the Heavenly Spheres completed by
1532. He spent the remaining 10 years of his life
collaborating with others on the topic, and debating
whether and when to publish. He saw the printed copy
on his deathbed.

The simple but hard to accept change was to put the sun
at the center of our solar system. With the earth one of
many planets orbiting the sun, the explanation for
retrograde motion became simpler and more accurate at
the same time.

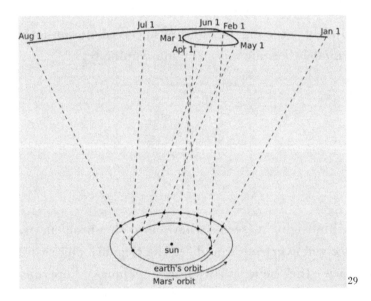

We are at this junction in the world of information
systems. The simple change of putting data at the center
of our enterprises will have a profound effect on the

---

29 https://bit.ly/2IIjqax.

flexibility, useability and economics of our information systems. While the change is simple, that doesn't mean it is easy or that it will be generally accepted.

How new ideas take hold

We are going to review several other major historical shifts to prime ourselves for what we are up against. As we shall see, merely having a better solution, merely demonstrating its efficacy, or having unassailable statistics is enough. But we also don't want to despair. All of these paradigm shifts ultimately took hold, but it is instructive to consider the tortuous path they took.

Round earth

In addition to the world being the center of the universe, it used to be flat. Up until the 1400s, sailors typically stayed close to shore – not a bad idea when you don't have a way to navigate in the open ocean. Europeans had known about the Far East for some time through trade over the silk road and the adventures of Marco Polo. Even the Portuguese sailing around Africa and arriving in India and the Spice Islands wasn't enough. It was still possible to cling onto the notion that the world was flat. Europe, Africa, and Asia were all on the same side.

Some wingnut named Christopher Columbus believed that the world was round. Round in a way that sailing west from Europe would land you in East Asia. He was right about the roundness, but somehow underestimated the circumference. Luckily, he did not sail off the end of the world. He discovered the Caribbean, thinking it was Indonesia. But that was good enough.

Within a few years dozens of people were sailing west. Kings and Queens were financing expeditions, captains were setting sail. They could have sailed west years earlier. Nothing had changed. There was no new technology. In this case, "existence proof" and the allure of vast riches was enough.

HEAVIER THAN AIR FLIGHT

The Wright brothers offer a slightly more nuanced example of proof leading to change. Most people at the turn of the previous century believed heavier than air flight to be impossible. Including one of the most notable, leading scientists of the day:

> *Heavier-than-air flying machines are impossible.*[30]

> Lord Kelvin, 1895

> (a short 8 years before Kitty Hawk)

This belief, of course, prevented them from investing time or money into such a venture. Despite dismissal of the idea by the mainstream, there were a few teams

---

[30] https://bit.ly/2IIOK9p.

working on the goal, including better-funded teams with real scientists instead of bicycle mechanics. In the same year that the Wright brothers made their storied first flight (1903), Stuart Pierpont Langley made two well-funded and very public attempts, both of which ended up on the bottom of the Potomac.

With that backdrop, one might think that a successful flight would garner some attention. On December 17, 1903, the Wright brothers made several flights on Kitty Hawk, ranging from their first flight at 120 feet to the furthest at 852 feet. The iconic photo was taken, and a press release sent to the Associated Press. It was summarily ignored. No paper covered this momentous occasion. At the end of that first day, a gale came up and wrecked their plane.

The Wrights returned to Dayton, Ohio, to continue work on perfecting their invention, primarily increasing range and maneuverability. In the whole of 1904, they made 152 flights of many miles, circles, and figure-eights returning to land and taking off again. For all of 1904, no one had yet even recreated their modest first flight. The world stayed away in droves.

How did the world find out about this adventure, and in very short order create a gigantic industry on top of it? In this case, the scoop went to a newsletter called "Gleanings on Bee Culture." We look back on breakthroughs like this and think surely someone would have noticed, might have been interested, but that wasn't the case.

But once the word finally got out, imitators sprang up almost immediately.

Copernicus, Columbus, and the Wright brothers give us one lens through which to view innovation, which shows us that our preconceived notions will often turn us away from looking at where the innovation would be.

I bring up the next two case studies to illustrate that even when a breakthrough has been proven, with scientific rigor, it can still languish. I bring this up because in order to save ourselves decades of unneeded suffering, we may need to look at what keeps people stuck and how the changes finally do emerge.

SCURVY

Throughout the 16th and 17th centuries, long distance sailing had become a major undertaking of commerce as well as war-making. But there was a dark side to the maritime industry: scurvy. Any voyage of more than a month was sure to be inflicted with an epidemic of scurvy, which was often fatal. More sailors died of scurvy (2 million) than both sides of the American Civil War. No one knew what caused scurvy, and for over 200 years there was a huge incentive to find out and prevent it.

In 1601 Captain James Lancaster performed an experiment on his voyage around Africa. One of his four boats was provisioned with lemon juice. By the time he reached Cape Hope, the sailors on the three boats without lemon juice were so sick, the sailors who had been taking the lemon juice had to sail the other ships to their destination.[31]

It's what happened next that puzzles me (really, what didn't happen next). One would think that anyone involved with this voyage (whether a survivor of the control group or the more fortunate test subjects) would insist on taking lemon juice their next voyage. One would think they would insist that their Captains provision it. Absent that, you would think they would bring their own. You only need a tablespoon a day, so a gallon would easily get you to the Spice Islands.

But this isn't what happened. For decades there was spotty adoption of this technique. Two or three generations of sailors would continue to go to sea and not die from getting tangled in the riggings or impaled on a pirate sword, but instead would lose their teeth and eventually their lives to a preventable disease of malnutrition.

Finally, in 1747 (nearly 150 years after Lancaster's experiment) the Physician James Lind conducted what is believed to be the first randomized clinical trial (on a

---

[31] https://bit.ly/2GkRpTO.

dozen sailors who were suffering from scurvy). His theory was that there were essential nutrients in food that were missing in the meager seafaring rations of the day. Most sailors lived on a diet of hardtack (dense unraised bread that kept for many months at sea), and occasional bits of dried beef. He believed in general that a more balanced diet, including fresh fruit and vegetables would provide the missing nutrients. For reasons that seem to be lost to history, we don't know why he chose lime juice for his proposed experiment, but he did. His findings weren't published until 1753. It was not until after Lind's death, in 1795 that the British made the provisioning of lime juice official policy.

Early in the Napoleonic Wars, Napoleon opted on a course to distract and distance the far superior navy of England. He decided that he could race their fleet to the Caribbean and the French Territory of Louisiana. By the time the British got there, they would be too sick to fight.

Little did he know that by this point (1804) the British were provisioning lime juice (hence the term "limeys"). When the flotilla arrived in the new world, the situation was the opposite of what Napoleon had hoped: the French were too ill to defend themselves, and the British made short work of them. Limes were also instrumental in Brittan's ability to blockade French ports, which helped with the decisive victory at Waterloo.

Even more incredibly, this news did not make it to the British merchant marines until 1865. Yet another 60 years.

HAND WASHING BEFORE THE GERM THEORY

Ignaz Semmelweis was a surgeon in Vienna from 1841-1855. He had noticed two disturbing trends: that women who gave birth in the major hospitals were far more likely to die from post-birth complications than those who gave birth at home and that no one seemed to be bothered by this state of affairs.

He noticed that the difference in rates of death by childbirth fever was even more acute in the teaching hospitals, such as the one he was working in. He noticed that surgeons would often go directly from dissecting a cadaver to attending a birth. Semmelweis conjectured that there might be something in or on the deceased patients' bodies and that the surgeons were inadvertently transferring to healthy mothers.

He devised an experiment to test his hypothesis, complete with measurements and a key performance indicator (death). His experiment was to have some of the surgeons wash their hands in a solution that contained a high concentration of chlorine as they transitioned from the morgue to the maternity ward.

These days we would bolster a study like this with statistical confidence intervals and the like. This was hardly necessary in his experiment.

The facing page contains a copy of the original mortality statistics.

Faced with this, you would think that his peers would thank him profusely, immediately adopt hand washing as the new normal, and "save" a large number of otherwise healthy patients. But this is not what happened at all.

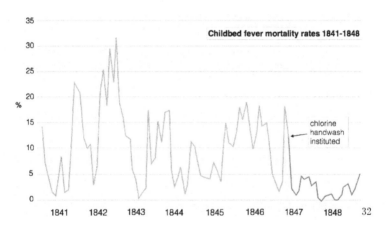

He was ridiculed and rejected. The established medical orthodoxy would have none of this. Semmelweis published his findings in 1847, and they began to have influence, but not at the Vienna General Hospital where he worked. He was drummed out.

---

[32] From https://bit.ly/29tNnH2.

He returned to Hungary, where he was from, and was able to recreate his impressive reduction in childbirth fever there as well. Again, it was not well received. In 1865, he was admitted to a mental institution where he died within a fortnight.

ULCERS

For most of the 20th century, ulcers were caused by excessive acid in the stomach, often caused by stress or spicy foods. The "cure" for this was antacids. While it was well known that bacteria and viruses caused many diseases, it was generally believed that none could survive the high acidity of the stomach, and so would not be responsible for something like an ulcer.

In 1982, Drs. Barry Marshall and Robin Warren of Perth, Western Australia, cultured the bacteria Helicobacter Pylori, taken from a patient's stomach, a patient with ulcers. Shortly thereafter Barry "proved" the causal connection between bacteria and ulcers when he ingested a culture of h. pylori and became violently sick within days. They also demonstrated that antibiotics were an effective cure.[33] In 2005, they were awarded the Nobel Prize for their work.

---

[33] https://bit.ly/2GnkxK1.

Non-linear Change

There are two kinds of change: those that improve on things that fit within the prevailing worldview, and those that require abandoning the prevailing worldview.

The former cases are easy, incremental, and uncontroversial. If you come up with a way to reduce packaging costs by 5% it will be rapidly adopted. If you can reduce the cycle time to build a car by 12 minutes, it will be embraced. If you can increase conversion rates on your web site by 10%, you will get a promotion and be emulated.

But if you come up with a way that improves things by hundreds of percentages, but at the cost of upending the status quo, you have a huge task ahead of you.

As obvious as the improvement might be, you may find yourself in the same position as Galileo Galilei, Captain Lancaster, or Ignaz Semmelweis: you might die before your idea becomes mainstream.

Perhaps as with Christopher Columbus, the Wright Brothers, or Marshall and Warren, you may live long enough to see the transition.

I can't tell how long this transition is going to take. It seems so completely obvious to me, but at the same time, I understand the power of inertia. Electric cars seem so obvious at this point (2019), and yet America is still less than 1% electric and is not behaving as if that number is about to change significantly (how much longer can we fund our roads on gasoline tax, when the electric vehicles are free riding?).

I bring all this up because it is helpful to prepare for the inevitable.

WHO IS NOT GOING TO HELP YOU WITH YOUR TRANSFORMATION?

I want to drive home the idea that merely being right is not enough. Proving you are right isn't even enough. Implementing something with demonstrable benefit isn't enough. The world wants to ignore anything that requires it to change its mind or habits.

Learning how to make this transition is the job of my next two books. Learning how to keep your organization from expelling the very change it needs is your job. I'm going to try to help in the rest of this chapter.

Historically, outside vendors had a vested interest in helping companies make a change, and they were handy allies. But this time is different.

THE REVOLUTION WILL NOT BE LED BY SOFTWARE VENDORS

Many of the key Information Technology transitions you've been through before were led by software vendors. The move to database-driven systems and application packages was driven by vendors, who charged for the acquisition of their products. The move to the Cloud and Software as a Service likewise are being propelled by vendors, who in this case are selling subscriptions.

There isn't a product or subscription-based service to sell in this space (at least not yet, that we know of). Don't expect vendors to push this. Instead, the adoption of Data-Centric methodology will be ruinous to the business models of these established companies.

THE REVOLUTION WILL NOT BE LED BY CONSULTANTS AND SYSTEMS INTEGRATORS

You might think that there would be a great deal of professional services work to be done migrating companies to this new approach. The large consulting and systems integration companies would be the logical parties to do this.

But they won't. Their business model is dependent on large, highly leveraged implementation and/or integration projects. One more mega project is worth more than converting 100 clients to Data-Centric systems. Furthermore, converting clients to Data-Centric systems makes those clients non-prospects for most of their current offerings.

THE REVOLUTION WILL NOT BE LED BY INTERNAL IT

Internal IT seems like a good possible ally — at least on the surface. In practice, most IT departments are so busy trying to keep the lights on and the data centers up and running, that they have little time and attention for breakthrough change. Our observation is that it is rare that internal IT can lead the charge (though it happens occasionally).

Sometimes the change starts in Enterprise Architecture (a logical place for it to start). But, if it doesn't get out of IT at some point, it faces a threat at each budget cycle.

DIGITAL TRANSFORMATION

It will be line of business (LOB) managers (or those they report to) who will lead this transformation because they will be the beneficiaries. As we mentioned earlier, almost all companies are in the midst of something they call "digital transformation." There is precious little consensus about just what constitutes "digital transformation," given that virtually everything about their information systems is already "digital."

Line of business managers have put up with a lot for the last two decades. Many of them suffered when their systems were outsourced, and as change orders became the new currency. Many are stymied by the byzantine and baroque tangle that is their current system architecture. Most firms started their digital transformation by retaking control of their web presence. This made and makes sense. The marketing department should be in control of the products and services they offer for sale, and more and more the website is where the offer lives.

Most of the definitions of "digital transformation" one finds on the web are very vague, and most make some disclaimer, such as, "Because digital transformation will look different for every company, it can be hard to pinpoint a definition that applies to all."[34] Many sites go on to define digital transformation in terms that line up with their current offerings. After providing a great deal of personal information, TechTarget offers to tell us, "What does 'digital transformation' really mean?"[35] but despite devoting 20 pages to the topic, fails to do so. There is a nice section that outlines the problem but precious little on what it is. If you are involved with digital transformation projects (about half of our projects over the last two years, have come in under the banner of "Digital Transformation"), you begin to see some patterns. The general themes are:

- Customer facing and/or customer self-service

- Fewer humans in the loop (automated decision making, and much better integration)

- Modern technology (Artificial Intelligence, Machine Learning, etc.)

---

[34] https://red.ht/2JuWEVV.

[35] https://bit.ly/2GnkYnD.

- Connected devices, especially the internet of things (see below).

One thing that is indisputable: this is a big deal, even if we can't figure out what it is exactly. IDC estimated the 2018 spend on Digital Transformation to be $1.3 Trillion[36] and projects it will represent $18 Trillion in additional business value by 2020, at which time Gartner says it will represent 36% of business' overall revenue.[37]

The emergence of Digital Transformation, which seems to be starting in the customer-facing areas of a business, is a beachhead for executives who wish to take control of IT.

If you have a Digital Transformation initiative in progress, it should be straightforward to attach the Data-Centric approach to the project and improve its outcome greatly.

Now that we have established who is and isn't going to be pushing for this revolution, we need to concentrate on ways to address the inevitable resistance. We know the resistance will be there, what follows are some thoughts about dealing with it.

---

[36] https://bit.ly/2EsnPbU.

[37] https://bit.ly/2kjq6Q4.

THE HERD

Let's face it, change among businesses is a herd phenomenon. On the savannah, staying with the herd is a survival technique. Fall too far behind the herd and you become prey. Getting too far ahead of the herd is equally problematic. Zigging when the herd zags is also a problem. That is not to say that the herd isn't moving. And the herd often changes direction. Members of the herd know to pay attention to subtle clues that signal the herd is changing direction.

In business, leaders track the herd through networks of their peers, through conferences and publications focused on their industry. They employ analysts and consultants to cross-pollinate and inform them of the changes afoot amongst their peers.

While this is a herd, it is also a business. Leaders know that correctly anticipating or at least rapidly reacting to the moves of the herd can be very profitable. The laggards are late to the watering holes and last dibs on the best new grazing.

As some members of the herd recognize, it is some of the very members of the herd that determine its future direction, even if it isn't done in a command and control fashion.

Armed with this information, we have three tactical responses:

1. Attempt to predict where the herd is going and get ahead, but not too far ahead.

2. Use your influence as a leading herd member to move the herd in a direction that will be to your advantage.

3. If you want your peers to buy-in, signal to them that the herd is moving in the direction you intend to go. Unlike on the savannah, in business, there is not nearly as much physicality to reinforce where the herd really is.

This may sound slightly cynical, but bear with me. Your firm, and your peers within your firm, will feel drawn to follow the herd. Right now, this includes embracing "digital transformation," amongst other things that may be specific to your industry. If you believe that a Data-Centric approach would be useful and necessary, then you want to figure out how to align it with where your herd is already headed.

SOCIAL PROOF

Related to the herd is the notion of social proof. If one person tells you something that is not entirely aligned with your current worldview, you will typically dismiss them. However, if several people in your sphere of influence are espousing similar messages, you may start to think they're on to something. People spouting identical dogma will usually be dismissed as some sort of ploy. But when different people express the same idea in different ways, we tend to listen to them, and to ultimately be swayed.

The first corollary to this is: one individual, whether internal or external, is not going to change an organization. It's not a scale issue, it has to do with how we process challenges to our status quo. A single challenge is dismissed. Many challenges eventually cause people to question their positions.

What this means for change agents is that the more people you can get subtly promoting the idea behind the change, the more likely the change will happen. Often this requires a combination of internal plus external agents. We have noticed that when we go into a firm, even with a handful of people, if we meet with decision makers independently and if they in turn are being fed by people we may have influenced, their receptivity is higher.

INCENTIVES

You can't pay people to adopt new behaviors. Indeed, many studies have shown that attempts to do so can yield the very opposite results. A day care center concerned about parents being perennially late to pick up their children decided to penalize late pickups with a fine.[38] The parents interpreted the fine as a fee for an additional service, and gladly paid the fee for the advantage of being able to pick their children up late. The fine had the opposite effect to that which was intended: more parents picked up their children later.

However, well-conceived incentives can have a huge positive impact. One thing we know is that even just tracking different metrics shifts attention and forms behavior. The gamification of just about everything demonstrates that just keeping track, keeping score, and offering recognition-based rewards can be powerful.

To be successful in using incentives to help with the paradigm shift we need to think deeply about what we measure. Right now, we measure return on investment for individual application projects. Really, we don't measure them, we project them. No one goes back after the fact and determines whether the factors that went into justifying the ROI of a project were achieved. But even if we did go back and measure, this is the wrong measure. This is measuring local optimization.

We need measurements that can measure progress toward becoming Data-Centric and not just determine the ROI of an individual project. We will return to this in the final chapter on governance. Once a Data-Centric initiative gets off the ground, the governance process will create metrics that help nudge people out of the status

---

[38] https://bit.ly/2V8VxzQ.

quo. For instance, if one of your governance metrics is reducing the total number of concepts being managed by the firm, a project that dramatically increases this number (and most application-centric projects would) would not be favorable.

The key incentives and the key measures are about whether you are making things better or worse. We use the term "datascape" to refer to the totality of the data under management at a firm. The "datascape" is described by its schema, in other words the metadata needed to understand the data. More schema means the datascape is more complex and therefore harder to understand.

The overall complexity of your "datascape" is a good indication of whether you are making things better or worse. The additions to complexity that a new project inflict on the firm needs to be weighed against the local ROI the project might (*might)* have generated.

You want to reward projects that decrease the overall complexity of your datascape. They may be application rationalization projects. They may be legacy modernization projects. Several of our clients are implementing what they call "data fabrics," which interposes a simpler data model in between new application development and the existing data stores. This is very much the right direction. However, you may need some additional metrics to measure this because, in the short term, it may look like it is increasing complexity (for the long interim you have all the existing data model complexity plus the much less complex complexity of the data fabric itself). The overall complexity doesn't go down until there is enough work on the data fabric that some legacy functionality can be abandoned.

CHAPTER SUMMARY

If you choose to adopt the Data-Centric paradigm, be aware that you will be flying in the face of incredible resistance. Most of the world, to say nothing of your own organization, will be arrayed against you.

It will behoove you to know that change of this variety is not achieved by merely proving that this alternative approach works. The move to Data-Centric, as with other major paradigm shifts, is different enough that a whole set of secondary immune responses will be marshaled against the change. Being prepared for the resistance and having tactics ready to counter this will be key to keeping the change going in face of resistance.

The following section introduces some firms who have successfully overcome their own resistance to becoming Data-Centric. They did this at a time when these ideas were far from mainstream. In some industries, these ideas are now coming closer to the mainstream. Regardless, it still behooves us to examine what they did to overcome resistance.

CHAPTER 7
Case Studies

The organizations examined in this chapter were able to successfully overcome initial resistance to change and embrace Data-Centric methodology.

S&P MARKET INTELLIGENCE

At \$2.4 billion,[39] S&P Market Intelligence (based out of Michigan) represents almost half of the revenue of Standard & Poor's. Their Data-Centric journey began with a small company called SNL, long before their involvement with S&P, but the ascendency of the data leadership in the S&P organization speaks volumes about

---

[39] https://bit.ly/2KQLNGl – page 32.

the strategic importance of this approach to not only the Market Intelligence Division, but perhaps to all of S&P.

HISTORY

The seed of S&P Market Intelligence was formed in the 1980s in a company called "SNL" (not Saturday Night Live, which was also founded around the same time, but a homophone for S&L – Savings and Loan, the industry for which they were providing information).

In the 1980s, SNL provided curated information on Banks and Thrifts for investors and potential acquirers. As this became self-sustainable and profitable, they expanded into adjacent markets, such as insurance, financial services, asset management, and real estate.

By the late 1990s, through mostly organic growth, they found themselves in over a half dozen industries, each with their own home-grown FoxPro database. FoxPro was a database with its own programming language, popular in the late 1980s and 1990s. There was a gradual recognition that this platform was not going to take them to their next level of growth.

THE ORIGIN OF DATA-CENTRIC METHODS AT S&P MI

In early 2000, they adopted Microsoft SQL as their next strategic Database Management platform. Prior to the conversion, they decided they needed to inventory the systems and particularly the databases they had created. As Hamish Brookeman, one of the architects at the time and who is still with the project, said, "Times of transformation are a great opportunity for positive change."

They built a database of database tables and columns which they called objects and items. The database helped them understand where some of the potential overlaps between divisions were. But they had another insight. Once they had a complete inventory of the database tables and columns that they had already implemented and were planning to migrate to MS SQL, it occurred to them that the new tables could be generated from the inventory they had created. They created a script that could read the metadata tables and generate a set of tables in the target architecture (in this case, MS SQL).

Their Data-Centric architecture has a very specific birthday: May 5, 2000. Their script created a log, so they have a record of every database so generated and the date on which it was born.

EVOLUTION

Shortly after the realization that new databases could be spawned from metadata (and therefore importantly that metadata could go from being descriptive to prescriptive), they sought and received senior management buy-in on an important policy. Henceforth, no new physical database tables would be created, save those that were generated from this metadata process. All databases were derived from a metadata core.

This simple and at the time perhaps innocuous decree has had a profound effect on systems at SNL and later S&P. By funneling all database creation through a single process, the Data Architecture group gained visibility on designs much earlier and more completely than they would have otherwise. And by knowing with confidence that the metadata was a 100% faithful projection of the production system, many more things became possible, and indeed became manifest. The metadata layer also had a memory of what physical databases had been spawned from the metadata.

THE ARCHITECTURE

This database of databases exists at the "logical level" by nature. Most application developers design their data models at the conceptual level. These are then recast (or "structurated," as some of our European clients say) into logical models, and finally translated one more time into the physical database tables in the specific vendor technologies.

The SNL data architecture team built a middleware layer based on the metadata. The middleware layer allowed user interfaces to write programs against an API that was populated from the logical model as represented in the metadata. The middleware translated requests into the physical layer for execution. In this fashion, applications became isolated and abstracted from the physical database. This would become significant, but not for several more years.

The edict "no databases would be created except through this generation process" was very significant. On the one hand, it greatly reduced the normal tendency toward rogue development and silo building. Without the ability to stand up a local database, many more systems came into the daylight. At the same time, it created the imperative that the data architecture group not unduly slow down the application teams. They realized if this became a burden either of excessive make work or delay of performance, the application teams would revolt.

The data architecture team kept up their end of the bargain. Over the ensuing 17 years, they have gone from a handful of "objects" (their term for the logical level classes) to over 8,000. They push changes from the metadata to development and from development to production on a four-hour schedule (and this can be expedited, if needs be).

They built what is essentially model-driven development of default form-based interfaces for all the objects. These are the primary data input means for most of the internal data users. These simple CRUD (create, read, update, and delete) forms were insufficient for the external consumers of their data, so another layer was built and code-named Hydra.

If you are a subscribing customer of S&P MI, the user interface you will see[40] is generated by Hydra. Hydra

---

[40] https://www.spglobal.com/marketintelligence/en/index.

provides a very rich, web-based user experience composed from reusable parts, with graphics, navigation, search, and the type of experience people expect from a modern browser-based UI.

While the use of the metadata-driven database creation is mandated, and therefore has achieved virtually 100% compliance, the use of the model-driven forms and hydra based UX are merely encouraged and have achieved approximately 40% and 90% adoption, respectively. All databases are generated and accessed through the middleware. No application has direct access to physical databases.

CORPORATE EVOLUTION

As we said, SNL grew organically and through small acquisitions through the 2000s. Their Data-Centric approach was crystalized in the ensuing 15 years. In 2015, they were acquired by Standard & Poor's and were rebranded as S&P Market Intelligence. The acquisitions and organic growth continued. The architecture continues to scale and extend with continued use.

As testament to the strategic importance of this approach, much of the data management team from SNL have been rapidly rising through the ranks of S&P and now hold senior management positions in the parent company.

As the original SNL group is being assimilated into the bigger S&P organization, more challenges are emerging.

They need to serve a much larger population of constituents, and they are encountering development groups that haven't grown up with this kind of discipline.

In addition to the challenges, the integration with the other divisions is providing some very interesting side-by-side comparisons of the two ways of building and deploying systems. The two divisions that are queued up to adopt this approach are S&P Ratings and Platts.

S&P MI is most like S&P Ratings, who primarily publish financial information augmented by the process of providing credit evaluation ratings for bonds and equities. The browser-based interfaces for Ratings are superficially similar to Market Intelligence. Platts, which is primarily focused on price assessment for commodities, has less overlap on the data side, but also has a similar editorial and publishing platform to support.

BENEFITS

The advantages of this approach show up in three main areas:

- Cost of Platform Migration
- Impact Analysis
- Cost of Application Change.

Cost of platform migration

One fortuitous benefit of funneling all updates through the middleware, came when it became strategically important to migrate to the cloud. The Market Intelligence Data Architecture team studied and architected their approach to this for over six months. Once the tradeoffs had been worked out, the implementation took just over a month. The platform migration became a one-time investment. All the 33 applications that are deployed on their middleware are automatically cloud ready. Once completed, any of the application then had essentially a one-click option to deploy to the cloud.

The same logic would hold if they ever chose to change database vendors. They would have one place to make the change and not 33 migrations.

In the other divisions, because each application was hosted on its own physical database, there was initially more options in their approach. Some of the high priority applications migrated more rapidly, as there was only a limited number of tables to be dereferenced. However, two problems became apparent in the other divisions. One was that the decision to go to the cloud was a migration not a reversible option. With MI, the physical target could be switched on and off. If they wanted to revert to on-premises, it was only a rebuild away. But in the other divisions, because the physical databases were directly accessed by the application code, once the application was changed, it was no longer possible to go back to the on-premise model. This was more potential problem than real problem as the decision to move had been made. The second implication was more significant.

Each application had to execute and manage their own migration. For the Market Intelligence group, once the migration had been made for one, it was available for all. For the other divisions, each application incurred essentially the same level of effort, repeatedly. The other divisions with more applications under management will probably be working through their cloud migration for many years to come.

Impact analysis

Impact analysis is the process one has to go through to determine how much a change is going to cost. Sometimes the change is required to comply with a regulation (such as the Sarbanes Oxley Act in the US or the GDPR in the EU), sometimes a change is to incorporate changes to reference data (a new country is recognized by the United Nations) and sometimes the change is one that the business wishes to introduce for efficiency or strategic reasons. Whatever the reason the first step is to determine how many applications, how many programs, how many database tables, how many APIs will be affected.

One example of a change that had to be evaluated and then implemented was the addition of South Sudan to the recognized list of countries in the world. For SNL the impact analysis was simple, they could run a single query and find all the applications that referenced their shared country table. Because all of them accessed the same table, and relied on the table, adding South Sudan to the table was all that was needed to implement the change. Far less than a days' worth of work.

Their sister company was much more like traditional enterprises. Lists of countries were scattered throughout their applications. In some cases they were hard coded as enumerated lists in programs. In other cases they were lists in XML documents, and there were many tables of countries (most of which were some mix of actual countries as well as marketing regions and the like). It took months just to do the impact analysis, and to get an estimate of the effort to change all the systems affected.

Cost of application change

Being able to measure and improve the cost of change of applications may be the most important metric that firms could manage. The firm that can implement functional changes rapidly is the firm that can evolve in place. The firm that cannot is fossilized and will spend disproportionately more to work around their lack of flexibility.

Very few companies have accurate comparable cost of change metrics. But at S&P, we were able to see anecdotal evidence that is very compelling.

Recall the South Sudan example a few paragraphs back. The cost to implement this change which was less than a person-day's work for MI has been a series of impact analysis and systems change that has cost the other divisions nearly $2 Million.

Because of the centralization of metadata (and reference data), SNL was able to include the addition of South Sudan in one of their routine monthly upgrades with virtually no additional cost. It was simultaneously available to all applications.

CHALLENGES

With successes have come many challenges for the S&P MI architecture. The main challenge is one of assimilation. The sister divisions that are being encouraged to adopt the platform are larger and have more numerous applications and application developers. The first challenge is just accommodating the newfound demand on the relatively small core team.

The second challenge is resistance. Each of the other divisions has developers and architects that have invested much of their careers in more traditional approaches. Their expertise and perceived value may be put at risk. It is human nature to resist change in such circumstances.

The third challenge is that some of the other divisions have invested in advanced technologies that have not yet been incorporated into the MI platform and will correctly perceive that they would literally be losing some advanced capability to adopt the platform.

S&P MI is in a good position with considerable senior management support for their approach, and they are aware that the longer-term success of their platform may well lie in partnering with their sister organizations to bring their advanced technology into the platform rather than making it an either-or proposition.

SUMMARY OF S&P STUDY

While it has not been definitively measured, the anecdotal evidence is that the MI Data-Centric approach is delivering up to 100-fold improvements in the cost of making changes to their applications. They have proven the stability of the platform by keeping it running and current for 18 years. They have proven its possibility by going from 7 applications and 140 objects in 2000 to 33 applications and 8800 objects in 2018.

SOKIL

The Sokil Group consists of six companies that provide transportation and logistics across Canada. It is a family run company that began with John Sokil and a team of horse-drawn wagons. The first of the Sokil Group to be registered, Edmonton Transfer, was incorporated in 1951. They have three primary locations across Canada. There are 200 employees, and almost as many truck tractors. They haul any type of cargo except liquids, such as petroleum.

Kim Sokil, a granddaughter of John Sokil, is the third generation of family to manage the firm. Kim has spent her entire career in IT. In the early part of her career she worked at Sokil for a few stints but then went off to a career that included Telecom, Medical systems, Government Agencies, and IT consulting. In that time, she had implemented many ERP and other packaged applications. She returned to Sokil in 2015 only to find that a system that she had helped implement in 1992 was still alive and kicking, but arguably past its shelf life.

That system was an IBM AS/400 system, originally based on a Transportation Management System package but highly modified. In the intervening 20+ years, the hardware had been upgraded once, but IBM had informed them that this was going to be the end of the line for that range.

So, Kim made one of her first priorities to move functionality from this system to a next generation system. One of her first decisions (that is shared a lot these days) was to get out of the business of managing computer hardware and move the system to the cloud. It was her second decision that started her on the path that ended in a case study in this book.

Kim decided she was not buying a package. This is still a minority decision, especially for someone in a small to medium business. I asked her why. She told me that in her consulting career, she had worked on a great many package implementations. In her experience, most didn't deliver the functionality that the client needed. They rarely completed on time and were poor value for the money. The base packages that most firms started with were rarely even close to the functionality needed.

Further, she said that once you commit to a package, you are on a rarely negotiable upgrade path. The vendor will provide upgrades, which are often disruptive, and if in the inevitable case that you modify the package, are no longer forward compatible. She knew enough to know what she didn't want.

She set out on a quest to find a vendor, a platform, an environment, or a set of tools where she could build and maintain the functionality she knew Sokil needed. Over the next six months, she engaged in over a dozen trial implementations. For each new product she tried, she would create a representative part of a solution, and explore how easy it was to build screens, reports, validation, and the like. Most were not up to her expectations.

Then she tried a product called AppSynergy from a company of the same name, which is bicoastally located in Florida and Washington State. The AppSynergy system is a model-driven, "no-code" or "low-code" environment, and while that wasn't what Kim was looking for specifically, she recognized its capability when she tried it out.

She started by building a manifesting system and a fuel management system, as these were the two systems most desperately in need of replacement. When these two systems smoothly entered production, she gained a great deal of confidence.

In 2016 she was convinced that this approach would allow her to convert all the systems from the aging hardware that they were currently using. She targeted a full conversion by spring of 2019 – at which point IBM would no longer support that model of AS/400. The scope of conversion included the following subsystems:

- Invoices –- system that automatically bills clients based on trip tickets.

- Integrated Freight Integration — API integration application that connected two servers together using Internet of Things (IoT) technology.

- Sales Reporting — a series of reports and dashboards for sales productivity.

- Delivery — an application used by the drivers to mark completed deliveries and capture electronic signatures (like UPS).

- Probills and Manifests — used by transportation industry to move goods, also sending customer emails of invoices and related documents.

- Warehouse Management — inventory capture information, including issues, receipts and cycle counting.

- Reports—a full suite of management reporting.

- Customer & Quote — system that tracked customer information and related quotes.

- HR & Payroll — simple information capture for resources, used to feed vendor payroll systems.

- Fleet Management — System that captured information on trucks including registration and vehicle maintenance.

- Customer Management — attached to their website so customers can self-serve. See delivery information, retrieve POD documents, invoices, and statements.

- Telematics—captured all the data recorded from GeoTab relays (e.g., engine data, trip data, driver safety data).

- Fuel Management — This system managed fuel consumption and handled data capture are needed for reporting taxes.

- Courier — This system managed they deliver small packages.

- Accounts Payable and Accounts Receivable—simple document capture.

- Content Management—they store all their scanned documents in the same database, indexed to the entities they correspond to.

She hadn't heard the term "Data-Centric," but that's exactly how her approach could be described. She said she had always had a philosophy of "data first" and was surprised that younger generations of application developers did not. These systems run on a single data model—a single, simple data model consisting of fewer than 50 tables. There is a very small amount of code (a few exception routines, triggers, and notifications need to be written in Java or JavaScript, but these are the exceptions). She is very intentionally avoiding writing code as much as possible, partly for maintainability and partly for those to whom she will eventually turn over the care and feeding of the system.

The system has all the attributes that we promote here, including ease of understanding and ease of change. I asked about the effort to make a routine change and a difficult change. By routine change, we agreed that something like adding a field to the database, getting that on a form, and providing formatting and validation would be a routine change. An example of a larger change would be something like adding a fuel surcharge feature, which might affect several modules, as it would have to be set up, maintained, and carried all the way through invoice calculation and reporting.

She said the routine changes typically take an hour or two, and she can slipstream them into production. She has enough experience with the system that she knows, which changes will not be disruptive. The platform is built such that these changes do not require data conversions, or even shutting the system down. A user of the system will get the change in the next refresh. The larger changes she said typically take 2-3 days.

I asked her to compare that with her experience with packaged implementations, and she laughed. Even the simplest of changes (e.g., to change the heading on a report) triggers a workflow of definition, quoting, scheduling, development, and more. Each step in this process typically takes weeks or longer to get from requirements into production.

Did I mention that all this functionality was built by Kim over the course of a few years? In my experience, traditional development would have a medium-sized team on each of the more than a dozen modules she has implemented over nearly that same time frame.

SUMMARY OF SOKIL STUDY

There are a couple of things I like about this case study. One is that it shows even medium-sized companies can benefit and benefit significantly from this approach. It shows that there are many ways to implement such an approach and that there are already third-party platforms that can take a lot of the hard work out of it. It also demonstrates that the Data-Centric approach delivers the promised value,.

Remember, our central criterion for describing something as "Data-Centric" is that all application functionality is based on a single, simple, shared core data model. This is exactly what is in place at Sokil.

CHAPTER SUMMARY

These two case studies are existence proof that it is possible, using technology that has been mainstream for decades, to build and maintain a suite of Data-Centric applications on a single shared core model.

These case studies (along with three others that I reviewed but was unable to get permission to share) share several other key attributes. My observations are generalization from all five of the companies I reviewed.

One is that they were built with very small teams, over relatively longish periods of time. None of these projects launched with a team seemingly big enough to implement even one application, and yet over time in each case, they implemented the functionality of dozens of applications.

Both of our case studies (S&P Market Intelligence and Sokil) had protection from very senior management. This type of endeavor is fragile to the onslaught of naysayers and people whose worldviews are threatened. At Sokil, it didn't hurt that the champion was a namesake and an heir apparent, but in each of the other cases, very senior management made sure the project was protected through its early development phases.

They all embraced model-driven development (low-code / no-code environments) to a greater or lesser extent. This is a curious observation, as neither the Data-Centric approach nor the low-code/no-code approaches demand model-driven development. Nonetheless, they do seem to co-occur.

They all seemed to find it amusing that traditional environments consumed most of their available resources on system integration and routine system changes.

Of the five case studies that were considered for this chapter, all but one (one I didn't write up) would do anything to avoid returning to a pre-Data-Centric world. The one firm that did revert did so because the cost of coordinating and sharing the one model as it became more complex, became more of a burden than they could handle. The others employed a combination of automation and dev ops combined with rigorous simplification.

As we will see in our second set of case studies, there are newer technologies that can help keep the model simple, and at the same time, allow easy extension and local specialization.

CHAPTER 8
Linked Data

The previous case studies prove that it is possible to become Data-Centric using traditional technology. This is the hard way to do it, although to put this in perspective even doing it this "easier" way will require a great deal of discipline over a long period of time.

Our observation is that the companies that have embraced Linked Data, Knowledge Graphs, and Semantic Technology have had an easier route to effective data-centrism. This section is to fill in just what is it about Linked Data that is different and helps with the migration to a Data-Centric approach.

Linked Data, Knowledge Graphs, and Semantic Technology share a lot of common characteristics. These three concepts can be defined briefly as such:

- Linked Data makes it easier to combine multiple datasets (even datasets that are not under your direct control) to express information.

- Knowledge Graphs are utilized by most of the digital native firms, including LinkedIn, Facebook, Google, and Twitter. A Knowledge Graph is a way to flexibly organize meaning in a way that is not manually intensive. There are many technologies for implementing a Knowledge Graph. The largest of the digital native firms have each invented their own, as it provides them with proprietary advantage.

- Semantic Technology refers to a set of standards for developing Linked Data and Knowledge Graphs. These standards were created by W3C, the same organization that built the standards powering the World Wide Web (including http, URLs, html, and the like). These standards, along with the variety of products that implement them, are collectively called "Semantic Technology," or alternatively, "The Semantic Web."

This chapter will focus on Linked Data concepts (many of which are implemented using Semantic Technology) and the power of "structure free" databases. Knowledge Graphs, and the rest of the Semantic Technology stack will be picked up next chapter. We will organize this discussion around the advantages that come with embracing these new approaches. We will also introduce specific technology or standards as we need to, to support the capability claims.

WHEN LINKED DATA AND SEMANTIC TECHNOLOGY BECOME DATA-CENTRIC

As we saw in our first two case studies, it is possible to become Data-Centric, with traditional data base and data modeling technology. However, there are some enabling technologies that make this far easier. I am becoming convinced that much of the success is not directly attributed to the new technology; rather, adopting the new technology encourages the mental shifts that are so important.

The new technology is a catalyst for the paradigm change. Sticking with technologies that are well known has a tendency to allow us to drift back into familiar patterns. The technologies we'll discuss in this chapter are just different enough to seem to be a big aid in making the transition.

Linked Data and Semantic Technology are not essential parts of a final solution, but Google's journey has been illustrative. Once upon a time, Google was a search engine. Owing to their commitment to a spartan home page, they didn't even have screen real estate for banner ads (which were one of the predominant sources of revenue in the early days of the web). In 2003 they acquired Applied Semantics,[41] which led them to Google Ad Sense. It has been touted as one of the best acquisitions of all time. It was this acquisition that broke them out of the search business and put them in the advertising business.

Then in 2010, Google acquired Metaweb, a company that combined Semantic Technology with the Linked Data that was available at the time. This included a product called "Freebase," which allowed users to reach beyond querying for keywords and into querying for meaning. Freebase was based on the W3C Semantic Web Standards. Google assimilated the team and the project and reworked it into the Google Knowledge Graph. This is the engine that powers the more sophisticated search results we've become familiar with. Google's Knowledge Graph, while originally seeded with the open Semantic Web standards, has been rebuilt with Google's proprietary infrastructure to handle the vast quantities of data under their control.

It's my personal theory that these acquisitions, and the embrace of a different technology stack, allowed Google to see things differently and embrace the paradigm shift. They have reimplemented their stack in their own proprietary technology and have left the standards behind, but I don't believe they would have arrived at the position they are in had they not adopted these approaches.

---

[41] https://bit.ly/2PjDMbm.

The technology described in this section is not exotic or proprietary. This technology has been in pragmatic adoption for over a decade. Most of the technology we will discuss is based on Semantic Web standards. The following solutions aren't the only way to solve each of the problems presented here, and we will present them in as general a fashion as possible, but this family of standards is quite coherent in solving the mostly intractable issues.

SEPARATING MEANING FROM STRUCTURE

One of the most profound advancements in the last two decades has been the ability to separate the meaning of information from its structure. In a traditional system, meaning is both horribly bound up in the data structure, and at the same time, not discoverable from it. Imagine a traditional system with a table of secret agents:

agent		
Id	Last Name	Full Name
006	Renton	Andy Renton
007	Bond	James Bond

There is nothing in this arrangement that would give the first clue as to what a secret agent is, other than the name of the table. But the name might just as likely been HMSS (Her Majesties Secret Service) or a German Acronym. The only person who might know what it means to be a member of this table is someone who read and interpreted the documentation.

In the next chapter, we introduce the more advanced aspects of Semantic Technology that provide machine-readable meaning, independent of structure.

A SINGLE STRUCTURE FOR EXPRESSING ALL DATA

In a relational database, each table is a new structure. In object-oriented, each class is a new structure. In big data, each dictionary and set of key/value pairs is a new structure. You must know the structure ahead of time to access the data, which is why these are called "structured databases." In semantically oriented systems, there is only one structure: the triple. Once you know the structure of a triple, you know the structure of all Linked Data and semantic databases.

A triple, not surprisingly, has three parts. It is a tiny sentence with a subject, a predicate, and an object.

Subject   Predicate   Object

The subject and object are nodes, the predicate is a named arc between them. It is also called an assertion because the triple can be read as a simple sentence that is an assertion (in the above, we assert that "Dave owns Semantic Arts").

As we'll see further on, all data and all information can be expressed as triples. We can harvest triples from unstructured data, and we can mine them from relational databases and big data stores. It gives us one unifying way to express what we know.

GRAPH DATABASES (TRIPLE STORES) FOR STRUCTURES

Conceptually you could think of a graph database or a triple store as a single relational database table with three columns: subject, predicate, and object. This isn't how they are implemented—there are several things done for performance and efficiency—but conceptually this is all there is.

There are two prevailing data structures in traditional applications: Object-Oriented Classes and Relational Tables. They both suffer from two problems:

1. They are rigid.

2. They must exist and be complete before any data can be created.

You cannot put rows in a table until the table has been created. You cannot add values to a table if the columns haven't been defined for that table. Data in a table is a cell at the intersection of a column and a row. Data in object-oriented is an attribute attached to an object that was created from a specific class. We are so accustomed to this that the alternative is a bit hard to think about.

Not all graph databases use open standards. Not all graph databases embrace Linked Data. Some graph databases, such as Neo4j, implement the idea of a database of triples, which they call nodes and edges. More precisely, two nodes joined by a directional arc.

Non-standards-based graph databases, such as Neo4j, have been free to invent some of their own conventions, some of which are quite handy for network style analytics. However, we are going to focus on the standards-based graph databases as they have an advantage when it comes to data integration and especially harmonizing data from many sources.

Both types of graph databases (standard and proprietary) take triples and assemble them into a "graph."

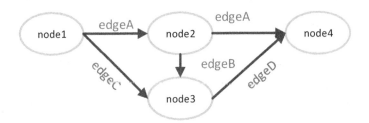

The power here is in the flexibility and evolvability. A node might have a dozen arcs radiating out from it. Maybe all the nodes of a certain type also have a dozen arcs radiating out from them. Then someone makes another assertion about one of the nodes. Now one of them has thirteen arcs radiating out. In relational or object-oriented systems, this is not done. Adding the possibility of a thirteenth "attribute" makes it available for all nodes. With a graph database, this is not a problem. This is how graph databases work.

RDF RESOURCE DESCRIPTION FRAMEWORK

The W3C standard way to describe a triple is covered in the RDF spec.[42] The RDF spec was adopted (in W3C terms, it was a "recommendation," which is the same status as HTML, HTTP, and URLs) in 1999.

The RDF spec outlines what you must do to be compliant. There are thousands of products compliant with RDF and hundreds of billions of triples that are free, open, and expressed in RDF. It will behoove you to at least take a look. As we said it is possible to implement a graph database that is not RDF compliant, but there are some pretty good reasons for at least considering the standards compliant route, not least of which is avoiding vendor lock in.

---

[42] https://bit.ly/2VeGaWr.

RDF covers what the nodes look like, what the triples look like, what types of triples can be expressed, several isomorphic ways to serialize triples, and a few other more arcane considerations (important when you get into implementation, but arcane for our purposes here).

GLOBAL IDENTIFIERS

All systems have identifiers. We create identifiers for employees, inventory items, contracts, and departments. We must do this to make systems work. But in traditional systems, all identifiers are local identifiers. In our secret agent example, a couple pages back, "007" only means "James Bond" if it is in the **Id** column in the agent table in Her Majesties Secret Service database.

deli		
Item	desc	price
006	Pastrami	$14.95
007	Ham Sandwich	$16.95

In the deli table, "007" could be a ham sandwich; in the tool crib system, a 9/16th inch socket.

These identifiers aren't just local; they are hyper-local. And because of this, there is a great deal of human knowledge needed to use these identifiers. Humans, mostly analysts writing queries or developers accessing data directly, must know and use the metadata in order to leverage the identifiers. They write "joins," which is how to say in a query language, "If the **Id** column in the agent table equals the **AssnTo** column in the gadget table, 'join' the two tables" (i.e., if "007" is in the **AssnTo** column, and you know this, you can find out who has the "Watch Garrote").

gadget				agent		
Weapon	Type	AssnTo		Id	Last Name	Full Name
006	Exploding Briefcase	007		006	Renton	Andy Renton
007	Watch Garrote	007		007	Bond	James Bond

It is important to note that the "007" in the Weapon column is not referring to James Bond, but the "007" in the **AssnTo** column is. This requires humans to have a priori knowledge of how these tables were constructed and how they are linked.

We are moving from structure being known and enforced ahead of time and recapitulated by analysts writing queries to reassemble data they know to being connected, to a world where the relations are implemented as they are discovered, without pre-established structure, and without humans stitching things back together.

It is the adoption of global IDs that finesses this. If each ID is unique in all the universe and means something, then it doesn't need database, table, and column qualifiers. If we have a global identifier for me, then we can make assertions about me without worrying about tables or columns.

The global IDs needn't be unique. They need only be unambiguous (e.g., if a global ID always refers to me, it is unambiguous). The fact that there may be more than one global identifier for me is a bit of a nuisance, but the technology still works (e.g., my employer may assign a global identifier to me, as might my hospital).

DEALING WITH NON-UNIQUE BUT UNAMBIGUOUS IDS

When executives get frustrated with managing and aligning multiple IDs for the same things, they will occasionally launch a project to implement a "universal ID." In other words, if many of your application systems use different IDs for the same patients, or vendors or products or employees or whatever, there is an impetus to change some of the systems to use one common identifier.

This is way harder than it sounds, and in the few times that it comes close to succeeding, it often gets undone when the firm decides to integrate with some external data source that has regrettably used some other identifier. We have worked with healthcare organizations where providers (physicians and nurses) typically have between a half dozen and a dozen identifiers each. Many of these are hardcoded into systems, are unable to change (e.g., the "EPICid"), and many more come from external agencies that assign identifiers (e.g., the DEA, the AMA).

The reason this is harder than it sounds is that the particular ID format, validation, storage, and assignment are deeply baked into the legacy systems that need to be changed. Each system to be changed can easily launch a million-dollar change project if it is feasible at all.

The alternative is to do four things:

1. Rationalize as many system identifiers as you can do economically. There are always some systems that can be changed for a relatively small effort without committing to a single set of identifiers. Getting to a limited number of identifiers makes the task more tractable.

2. Implement an identity management service. This will be a central topic of the third book in this trilogy, <u>Data-Centric Architecture.</u> For now, just understand that a portion of your architecture should understand what uniquely identifies things. This layer can intercept new record creation, providing existing IDs and maintain aliases whenever they are known.

3. Implement "sameAs." When you discover that there are two global identifiers for the same real-world "thing" (e.g., the company, "Semantic Arts"), which can easily come about because each company seems to assign a new identifier to us, it is not a show stopper. We merely employ another (special) predicate called, "sameAs," and

construct a triple that asserts that the one identifier is referring to the same thing as the other identifier. Standards compliant systems know that this means anything we know about one are now known about the other.

4. Once asserted (or inferred, as we'll discuss soon), the system will consider all facts associated with one identifier to be combinable with all the facts associated with the other identifier.

SELF-ASSEMBLING DATA

Global Identifiers gives us an interesting emergent property: self-assembling data structures.

With traditional data structures, humans do all the assembly. In a relational database, analysts write "joins" in their queries to assemble data from more than one table. In object-oriented development, the equivalents to "joins" are managed by programmers. In big data and document-oriented databases, the equivalents of "joins" are performed by Data Scientists assembling data from multiple sources.

With global Ids and a graph database, the system does the joins for you. If we acquire a new factoid about James Bond, provided we associate that factoid with the same global ID, the system will snap it all together. Humans aren't writing code or queries to assemble the data.

There is still some work to be done. In this world, queries exist, but they exist to define the subset of data of interest for a particular use case and not to build the connected data.

RESOLVABLE IDS

A graph database works regardless of whether you know what the IDs "mean." However, you will find much greater utility in a graph database if you can resolve the global ID and find out what it refers to.

One type of global identifier called the "guid" is not quite as useful as what RDF the semantic web community has adopted. A guid is an identifier that is mathematically determined to be globally unique. For instance:

359d3847-f947-438a-90b7-3b073f3fcc83

The above collection of characters is a guid I just generated at https://www.guidgenerator.com/. I could use this identifier to refer to something, but if I sent it to you, you would have no way of knowing what it means, and nowhere to go to find out more.

And because of that, the opportunity for creating many guids representing the same real-world thing are legion.

Instead, the Semantic Web community has adopted the best practice of basing global IDs on name spaces, which in turn are based on the domain name system. These identifiers are called URIs (Uniform Resource Identifiers) and, as we'll see, are very analogous to URLs (Uniform Resource Locator). It is more proper and inclusive to use the term IRI (International Resource Identifier), which includes identifiers that can be made up from Unicode characters, and therefore could be in non-western character sets such as Chinese or Russian.

The domain name system is the infrastructure that ensures that when you type something like www.semanticarts.com into your browser you are directed to a server and a set of web pages that we control. The idea of a namespace was introduced with XML, the primary intent to be to prevent name clashes by qualifying identifiers.

Best practices for namespace construction in Semantic Technology bases namespaces on domain names. For instance, one of the namespaces that Semantic Arts controls is http://ontologies.semanticarts.com/gist/.

http://ontologies.semanticarts.com/gist/

Namespace

Because we own the domain name (semanticarts.com), we can create subdomains (ontologies) and further path qualifiers (/gist). Any term we put after the last slash is globally unique (as long as we don't screw up). Whether it is a class (http://ontologies.semanticarts.com/gist/Person) or an instance (http://data.semanticarts.com/SemArts/_person_6), these are globally unique identifiers. And if we choose to, we can easily make them resolvable (subject to security constraints). We make each of these identifiers resolvable as if it were a URL. That is, if you type it in your browser bar, we can generate a page that defines it or potentially tells you what we know about this item that we choose to share.

FOLLOW YOUR NOSE

In RDF data, most of the data is URIs. All of the "subjects," all of the "predicates" and many of the "objects" (those that aren't literals) are URIs. What this means is they are potentially resolvable (based on security constraints and whether the creator of the URI provided a resolution mechanism).

That means when you query for some data, you can click on any of the returned items, and it will display, as appropriate, what data is going to be revealed (to you). Because all the data is triples, you could click on any predicate and find out what it means or click on any object and find out what other properties are attached to it.

This style of exploring through a dataset that you have little or no prior knowledge of it called "following your nose." This is in contrast with traditional relational databases, where in order to query anything, you must have pre-existing knowledge of the schema.

QUERYING A TRIPLE STORE

A graph database needs a query language. You rarely want to deal with all the data in the database at once. Proprietary graph databases have their own query languages, including some that are becoming de facto standards, such as GraphQL or Cypher. The semantic web stack has SPARQL. SPARQL is syntactically similar to SQL (the query language for relational databases), which is unfortunate. In a relational system, most of the query writing energy goes into composing the "joins" or describing how data from one table will be combined with data from another. This is unnecessary in semantic databases, as the URI / global ID does the joins for you. In SPARQL, the query language is mostly about describing what subset of the graph you are interested in. Therefore, equivalent SPARQL queries are usually 10-20% as verbose as their SQL equivalents.

LINKED DATA

Which brings us to one of the more interesting, and additional emergent properties: the possibility of what is called "Linked Data," which comes in at least two varieties: "Linked Open Data" and "Linked Enterprise Data."

Linked Open Data (LOD) came into existence in 2007 through a combined effort of the University of Berlin and OpenLink Software. What the project did was extract all the information from the "InfoBoxes" on Wikipedia (those sidebars with organized factoids on the right of many pages). The organizers noticed that the info boxes, which were essentially label/value pairs, could be easily converted into triples, where the subject was the topic of the page, the predicate the label and the object the value.

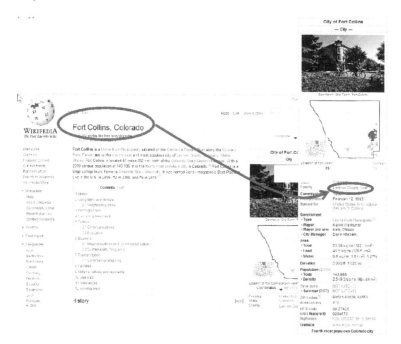

As of this writing, the corpus is 438 million triples. These triples are all expressed in RDF with URIs as identifiers. They are stored in a graph database, which is publicly available at: http://dbpedia.org/sparql (courtesy of OpenLink).

Anyone can go to this endpoint and execute queries against the DBpedia triple store.

After a while purveyors of other data sources recognized that with just a little after-the-fact coordination, they could link their data with the DBpedia data. A few of the early and representative datasets to align with DBpedia were the CIA World Fact Book and GeoNames.

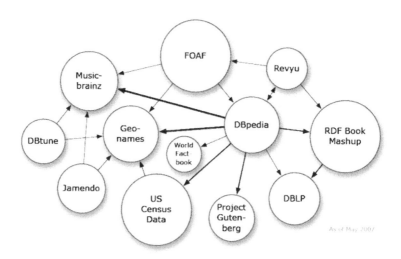

Each of these had curated data, the first primarily about countries and their histories, leaders, people, economies, and the like. GeoNames has a wealth of information about individual geographical features on the earth, everything from mountains and rivers to cities and states. Some of each of these datasets have overlapping information with DBpedia and each other.

By declaring that the GeoNames URI for France (http://sws.geonames.org/3017382/) represented the same concept as DBpedia's (http://dbpedia.org/resource/France), as well as the New York Times (http://data.nytimes.com/67127587134490296321), anyone with access to all three datasets could get the sum total of what all of them knew using the "sameAs" we discussed prior, without doing data integration, or conversions, or any of the traditional high labor approaches to integrating information. This is the "link" in Linked Data.

As more and more datasets got wind of the potential, more became aligned. To be clear, you don't need total agreement to be aligned. Relatively modest alignment creates great leverage.

There are now hundreds of billions of triples that are loosely affiliated (many require registration, and some are not always available), but it shows the potential and scope. This is referred to as the LOD cloud, and you can track its progress here https://lod-cloud.net/.

By 2009 there were 89 Linked Data datasets:

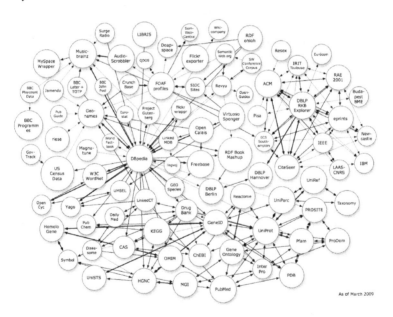

By 2014 the number had grown to 570:

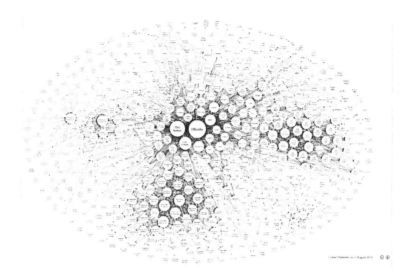

And now, even with the use of color, the 1,186 datasets in the LOD cloud are a wealth of mostly free data waiting to be combined with your data. The pink region here represents life sciences data, which includes, among other things, the entire human genome.

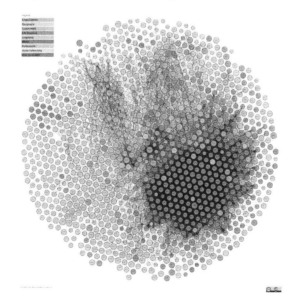

And enterprises have realized, by analogy, they could do the same with their own information internally. Much of it they don't intend to make public, but the value of sharing it internally is obvious and profound.

All you really need to integrate a great deal of data in an enterprise is a commitment to common standards, and a way to either use the same URIs (or where this is not possible, to be able to declare when two URIs refer to the same thing).

CHAPTER SUMMARY

The LOD movement, catalyzed by DBpedia, provides an example of what is possible by adopting a few simple changes to the way we think about organizing and identifying information.

Traditional relational database systems are based on hyperlocal identifiers that rely on human knowledge at query time in order to construct even the simplest data join. By contrast, Linked Data relies on global identifiers, which have constant meaning independent of context or location. This allows for self-assembling data, taking the human out of the business of writing joins in queries.

Having the identifiers double as valid URLs means that resolution, and therefore understanding or further exploration, is just a mouse click away.

Hopefully, the massive growth of the LOD cloud should inspire enterprise advocates as to what is possible, with just the lightest touch of governance.

But Linked Data is the tip of the semantic iceberg. In the next section, we explore how this technology stack allows us to express meaning, and how this in turn encourages economy of expression.

CHAPTER 9
Ontologies, Knowledge Graphs, and Semantic Technology

Ontologies are conceptual models built using Semantic Technology. They provide a layer of meaning on top of Linked Data and graph databases.

Our observation is, and our earlier case studies demonstrate, that it is possible to establish a Data-Centric enterprise using traditional technology. We have also found a much easier route, combining Linked Data concepts from the previous chapter, which Semantic Technology, which we will cover here.

We have found benefits in two major areas, from the adoption of Semantic Technology:

- Implementation Benefits – Adopting Semantic Technology design and infrastructure provides a number of direct implementation benefits, including reducing complexity of data models, and increasing flexibility of delivered systems.

- Perspective Benefits – Even without the implementation benefits, merely reframing the problem and forcing yourself to look at the enterprise application problems through the lens of semantics, often is enough to shift your point of view. Seeing the problem differently is often a prime benefit.

What follows is a very high level review of some of the differences introduced when you adopt Semantic Technology.

METADATA IS TRIPLES AS WELL

In most systems, data and metadata are very different things:

- *Data* comprises the specific facts about individual instances, such as "the price of product 23 is $17."

- *Metadata* comprises the data that defines the structure and meaning of data, such as "the Inventory table contains columns for product IDs and prices."

In relational technology, metadata is expressed in Data Definition Language (DDL) and data is expressed in Data Manipulation Language (DML).

In semantically based systems, data and metadata are all just triples. A single triple tells us that "Person" is a class (this is metadata).

Another triple tells us that "Dave" is a "Person." (connecting data to metadata – note this loose and late binding relationship of data to metadata is one of the distinguishing features of semantic based systems.)

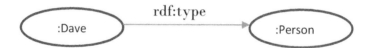

One flexibility that we get from this is that with one more triple, "Dave" is an "Employee," and with another, "Dave" is a "Patient." We don't need new identifiers, we just make a single assertion, and Dave is a member of many classes, simultaneously. In relational technology, an instance is only a member of one class (a row is only in one table). There is incredible flexibility in this simple approach of allowing an instance to be in many classes simultaneously.

The other interesting side effect of having metadata be expressed in the same way as data, we can freely mix data and metadata, giving a way to discover what things mean, without having to know a priori.

If we take the "follow your nose" approach from the previous section and now apply it to a triple store that has metadata loaded, we can follow our nose from an individual (instance) to its class. We can find out what type of thing it is (its class). Let's say we run a query that returns ":dave" as one of the URIs in a triple; we might click on :dave to get a page that tells us some of the key attributes of :dave, including his class memberships. We may find that: dave is an ":Employee," a ":Consultant," and a ":Parent." Clicking on any of these will tell us what they mean.

FORMAL DEFINITIONS

A formal definition is one where a software system can infer class membership based on the models plus the data.

A partial formal definition is one where we can infer data based on known class membership. For instance, if part of the definition of being a person is that they have a birthdate, then a system can infer a person has a birthdate, even if that date is unknown.

As we said, a complete formal definition is one where there is enough information in order to infer membership into a class, based on data in the database. Let's say the formal definition of a Patient is as follows:

A Patient is a Person who has received diagnostic or therapeutic services from a healthcare provider.

Therefore, a system can infer membership in the class of Patients for any Persons that have had such services. In an ontology editor, like Protégé, this would look like this:

Description: gist:Patient

Equivalent To ⊕

gist:Person and **gist:hasReceived** some
(gist:TherapeuticServices or **gist:DiagnosticServices)**

Serialized as OWL it looks like this:

```
Class: gist:Patient
 EquivalentTo:
 gist:Person
 and (gist:hasReceived some
 (gist:DiagnosticServices or
gist:TherapeuticServices))
```

Imagine that we found the following assertions (and they may have been from the web, an unstructured document, or a structured database):

Joe Jones had his gunshot wound repaired at St Luke's.

If a system can establish:

- that Joe Jones is a Person,

- that gunshot wound repair is a treatment (CPT code 27033, for those who are curious), and

- that St Luke's is a medical facility,

then

- the system can conclude (or infer) that Joe Jones is a patient.

A complete definition is one where we don't need to assert membership in a class, the system can do it for us. In the previous examples, Person was a partial definition, and Patient was a complete definition.

At first, this doesn't sound like such a big deal, but it has surprising implications. The first is that it removes ambiguity from class definitions. In the past, the definition of a class or table was generally in the documentation, and almost always underspecified (if it existed at all). It was assumed that everyone (users and programmers) knew what all the classes and tables meant. Most traditional systems have thousands of classes and tables, many have tens of thousands. Very few people understand even a fraction of these well.

Having more complete definitions means there is lower cognitive load on the users and developers. They only really need to understand and agree with the formal definitions and the concepts from which they were constructed. While this is still a bit of work, we routinely see order of magnitude reductions in complexity, and often two orders of magnitude reductions.

SELF-DESCRIBING DATA

In a semantic system, the data and the metadata that describe the data is co-located. What this means is that when you run a query and encounter a property or attribute or data value that you are not familiar with, you can, in a well-designed environment, click on the item and understand what it means and what else it is connected to. If you were searching for roller coasters in DBPedia (using SPARQL), you would query the following:

```
SELECT ?rc

WHERE {

?rc RDF:type dbo:RollerCoaster .}

LIMIT 100
```

The query yields a list, the first five of which appear below. Note that these are all URIs (globally unique identifiers).

rc
http://dbpedia.org/resource/Firehawk_(roller_coaster)
http://dbpedia.org/resource/Behemoth_(roller_coaster)
http://dbpedia.org/resource/Cannibal_(roller_coaster)
http://dbpedia.org/resource/Mad_Mouse_(Michigan's_Adventure)
http://dbpedia.org/resource/Mad_Mouse_(Pavilion)

Clicking on one of these (Behemoth) gives us a new page with a set of formatted data, including, for example, these tidbits about the Behemoth roller coaster:

dbp:cost	• C$26 million est.
dbp:dropFt	• 230 (xsd:integer)
dbp:duration	• 190.0

If you didn't know what "dbp:dropFt" was, you could
click on it and get a definition (in principle, at least). We
used to use this example in our training class, and the
property was called "verticalDrop." Now the property is
"dropFt," but I'm pretty sure it's the same data. In
other words, it answers the question, what is the largest
single drop in the course of the roller coaster?

The point is, with a traditional system, you need to know
all the structure, all the terms, and what everything
means, even before you execute your first query.

In a semantic system, you can execute a very naïve
query, and when you see things you weren't expecting or
don't know, you can click on them (if the system is well
designed) and find out what they mean.

SCHEMA LATER

There is a huge debate now between "schema on write"
and "schema on read." "Schema on write" means you
must know all of the schema before you write anything
to the database. In other words, all the tables and all the
structure must be present before you do any writing (or

reading). All relational and object-oriented systems are "schema on write" (i.e., the schema must exist before data can be written).

"Schema on read" says we will figure out the schema as we go. Go ahead and put the data in the data lake with whatever keys and tags you'd like, and the data scientists will work it out later.

Both approaches are flawed. The former slows people down because as new data is discovered, there is a considerable lag before the data administrators have set up the structures to handle the new data. This delay is becoming less and less palatable.

The latter approach means the only people who know (sort of) what the data means are the data scientists who have plumbed the depths of the data. But there are two problems with this: 1) each data scientist may come to a different conclusion, and 2) any conclusion they come to is unlikely to be shared with anyone else.

With Semantic Technology schema can be added as it is uncovered or designed. Imagine a genealogy triple store that only had two properties: "hasParent" and "gender." From this, you could define the class of all "mothers" and "fathers" and infer people into them. You could define the class of "grandparents" as well as "grandmothers" and "grandfathers." We can derive ancestor from parent. We can define the class of "uncles" and specific uncle relationships. All of this is schema that can be added long after the data has all been created.

OPEN WORLD

As Tim Berners-Lee has so often said, on the Web and on the Semantic Web, "anybody can say anything about anything." This doesn't resonate in our enterprises. But before we throw the baby out with the bathwater, let's dig a bit deeper about why the Semantic Web is the way it is and how to have the best of both worlds.

The Semantic Web is predicated on the idea that you will continually be harvesting and accreting additional information. Therefore, at any point in time, the information you have will be incomplete. There is a great deal of reasoning you can do with incomplete information, but there are limits. For instance, if my municipality's definition of an impoundable vehicle is one with more than five parking violations, then once I discover five parking violations, I can infer that the vehicle is impoundable. New information will not reverse that inference.

The converse is not true. If I find a vehicle with three parking violations, I cannot conclude that it is not impoundable. The open world, and the recognition that we are always dealing with incomplete data, conspire to tell us that if we look a bit harder, we may find some more parking violations.

This runs counter to what most corporate developers are accustomed to. It is one of the lynchpins of the ability to evolve a database in place. The more productive thing to do is embrace this open idea, and use the closed world assumption as an exception, when one needs to. The semantic query language, SPARQL, which we alluded to above, allows us to make conclusions based on the data at hand. You can write a query that concludes, based on what we know now; this is not an impoundable vehicle.

LOCAL CONSTRAINTS

Many developers and database designers come to Semantic Technology feeling dismayed at the seeming lack of constraints, and they sometimes leave the approach for that reason. Some adopt design approaches that mimic what they are used to but compromise the potential of the Semantic approach.

The lack of constraints is tied in with the open world. It essentially says, "I'd rather have partial information than no information." A system with constraints essentially says, "by rejecting incomplete information, I'm saying I would rather have no data than incomplete data." Most constraints are completeness checks: all items in this table must have values for these five columns.

Let's say that our definition of Employee (US Employee) said semantically, "all employees have birthdates and social security numbers." If we declared someone an Employee in a semantic system, we would know that they have a birthdate and a social security number, even if we don't know what those values are. A traditional system with constraints would reject the assertion that someone is an employee if there wasn't a birthdate and social security number to come along with it.

There is now a standard to allow us to add constraints to a semantic system, and that standard is called SHACL. SHACL has been designed in a way that the constraints can be applied locally. We can have two triple stores (two "repositories" in the lingo) that were built based on a shared ontology, and because of that, they have a shared definition of meaning. One, the "curated" repository, could have constraints applied, such that a set of information in that repository is either complete or missing. Any Person data in the Employee repository would only be there if it had a birthdate, a social security number, and perhaps a start date and a pay rate. Another repository might have Patient data and would only have a record if we had patient ID, date of birth, gender, and at least one payment method. A third repository could just have whatever information we have on people.

If we needed a curated set of data, we could interrogate either the employee repository or the patient repository. In each case, we would get incomplete information relative to what we might know about a person if we interrogated all three repositories, which we would get a complete picture.

We think this ability to have global shared definitions, based on open world principles, coupled with the ability to have repositories with locally enforced constraints, is the best of both worlds.

CURATED AND UNCURATED DATA

There is a tension in the semantic web community between the wild west notions of the open world assumption and the desire for enterprises to "button things down." This often leads to two separate sets of databases, one that is mined by data scientists that are populated with data that is gathered from a myriad of sources and of course has low consistency and quality (though it might contain interesting insights not available to the corporate systems). The other is the highly curated and controlled enterprise data.

But these two need not be polar opposites. Both can be expressed in a shared ontology. In other words, the meaning of Person or Employee might be equivalent even though the rules of enforcement in one database are strict and another lax.

What this does is if you have a business problem that only needs or wants curated data (e.g., your internal payroll system), you should probably only use the curated dataset. But you may have an application that would benefit from the combination or curated and open data. Maybe combining your internal curated data about your employees from open data harvested from the web would lead to some interesting insight. This is made far easier if the curated and "uncurated" datasets share a single ontology (i.e. if the concepts mean the same thing even though the rules of consistency are not necessarily enforced consistently in both).

ONTOLOGIES

An ontology is a conceptual model, built using a formal modeling notation. We will use the OWL modeling language as defined by the W3C as the canonical example, although there are other modeling languages.

For those who wish to delve deeper, one of our colleagues at Semantic Arts, Michael Uschold, has written a very approachable and yet deep treatment of OWL: Demystifying OWL for the Enterprise.[43]

Technically any data expressed in this modeling notation and packaged in an appropriate wrapper is an ontology. This would include a file of instance level assertions as long as it was packaged as an ontology; however, when most people use the term "ontology", they are referring to the definition of the classes and properties that make up the model.

---

[43] https://amzn.to/2ItJFSY.

The triples that make up the formal definition of the meaning of the classes and properties are called "axioms."

An ontology is different from traditional conceptual models in at least three important ways:

1. It is computable. That is, you can execute code (reasoners) against the ontology.

2. The use of the reasoner can detect logical inconsistencies in a way that other conceptual models cannot.

3. It can be directly implemented. Traditional conceptual models must be transformed into logical models and then physical models before any data can be captured and stored. The ontology can be loaded as is into a triplestore, and data can also be loaded conforming to the ontology and be ready to be used.

MODULARITY AND REUSE

Ontologies have an interesting property of being modular. This modularity allows for partitioning of a domain into comprehendible sized chunks. One ontology can import another, which means it brings in the declaration of the classes and properties, as well as the axioms that make up the formal definitions. The importing ontology has all the concepts from the ontology it imported and can start extending from there.

Imagine you were in the business of selling chemical substances. You might arrange your ontologies like the example shown below. The materials ontology knows about and extends the chemical ontology but need not be concerned with the price of materials. There is surprising economy in this approach. Often each module in a scheme like this may only have a few dozen to a hundred concepts. This is small enough that most consumers of the ontology can understand it.

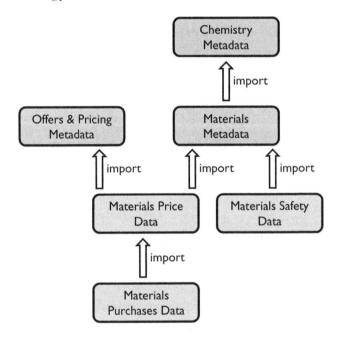

This chunking into modules is a great boon for reuse. The first boon for reuse is getting each ontology to an understandable size. The related boon to reuse is that sometimes an ontology has axioms that conflict with the importing ontology. Having reasonably sized modules allows an importer to select the modules they want and avoid axioms they don't want.

SELF-POLICING DATA

In a traditional system, the protection of a data set falls to the application that maintains it. But this makes the data very dependent on the application, encouraging further creation of data silos.

As we move to the Data-Centric model, we uncover the need for data to police itself (i.e., take care of its own quality management, constraints, and security).

This cannot be achieved by standards alone. The standards give us most of the building blocks we need, but some architecture is required to implement them. As mentioned earlier, this process will be more closely examined in <u>The Data-centric Architecture</u>, a companion book to this volume. For our purposes here, it suffices to say that when a certain architecture is Data-Centric, it is independent of any application managing data, based on rules (also expressed in data) that co-exist with the data.

COMPUTABLE MODELS

Traditional systems have data models as well. Often, they have conceptual models, logical models, and physical models. There is a difference in kind between ontologies and traditional models; we call that difference, "being computable."

It is very analogous to the difference between a paper map and an electronic map, such as Google Maps. They are both models of the real, geospatial world. The difference isn't level of detail—a paper map can have any amount of detail. The difference is that one (Google Maps) is a computable model. You can interrogate the model, ask how far two points are from each other, how to get from here to there, and how many coffee shops are on the route.

You can ask a paper map the best route from point A to point B, but it is not going to help you. Google Maps is a computable model of geography.

The analogy holds between traditional data models and next generation data models. A traditional relational model, even though it may have been built with electronic tools, cannot be interrogated in any deep sense. There are a wide number of queries that can be executed against a next generation data model. It can work out its own class hierarchy, spot logical inconsistencies, infer instances into classes, and determine classes that are closely related. The computable model can be used to generate other models.

INTEGRATION WITH RELATIONAL

You won't put all your data in a semantic graph database (at least, not in the short- to medium-term). Most of your existing data will persist in relational databases. However, we can achieve most of the benefits of a Data-Centric architecture without re-platforming the relational data.

The secret to this is a combination between a mapping technology called Relational to RDF Mapping Language (R2RML) and the ability to federate queries.

R2RML is a W3C standard that describes how to create a map between a relational database and RDF triples. The map essentially describes how to mint URIs from the relational keys and establishes the equivalency between the column names and semantic properties. The fascinating thing about this standard is once the map is built it can be run in either of two modes. In "ETL" (Extract, Transform and Load) mode, it mimics the behavior of the utilities that have been populating data warehouses for the last several decades. You process the entire database and turn it into triples which can then be loaded into a triple store.

The same maps can be used in a federated query mode. In the federated query mode, a semantic query uses the R2RML map to reach into the relational system at query time and only "triplify" (or transform into triples) the datasets it needs. This is typically combined with query results either from a map to another relational database or to a triple store. This process of combining data from multiple data stores is called "federation." The ability to combine triples stored in a triple store with those dynamically discovered at query time is a unique feature of this technology stack and is a key part of most migration strategies.

INTEGRATION WITH BIG DATA

In an analogous fashion, the semantic web standards provide a way to reach into "big data." Most big data these days is expressed in JavaScript Object Notation (json) syntax. The data is in "documents" (these are not like word documents; these documents are nested sets of dictionaries and arrays). In json, a dictionary is syntactically expressed within { } and has keys followed by values (e.g., { *'hasCapital': 'Denver'*}) and an array is comma delimitated in [ ] (e.g., *['Mon', 'Tue', 'Wed', 'Thu', 'Fri', 'Sat', 'Sun']*). It turns out that programmers and data scientists can deal with these structures very easily, no matter how deeply they are nested (for instance, you can, and usually do, have dictionaries of dictionaries with arrays of dictionaries).

While a programmer or a data scientist may be able to parse these structures, the problem is there is no mechanism to integrate this data with anything else you might have. This is where another standard, json for Linked Data (JSON-LD), comes in. It is essentially a map from semantics to json data structures. It is implemented as a header to a json document that maps the keys to semantic properties and describes how URIs will be minted.

Again, this allows you to either convert json data to triples and store them in a triple store or leave them where they are and interrogate them semantically at query time.

NATURAL LANGUAGE PROCESSING

For about two decades the holy grail of integration has been the integration of structured (relational) with unstructured (natural language documents) data. This has been a very hard problem for a long time. It is now a medium hard problem. Many people have solved it, and the general solution is within reach.

Natural Language Processing (NLP) has been pretty good at extracting "named entities" from documents for a long time. A "named entity" is something like a specific person, organization, place, transaction, or event. What NLP has not been very good at—which is to say it required a lot of computational linguists to spend a lot of time training and tuning—is finding the relationships between the named entities in a document. We are entering an era where this is doable and possible (with a bit of training and configuration) to align the relations expressed in a document with the relations (properties) in an ontology. What this means, is it is now possible to harvest triples from unstructured documents that conform to an ontology, and therefore harvest data from documents that can be combined with structured data.

SEMANTIC STANDARDS STACK

This is a variation of the "Semantic Web Layer Cake,"[44] which was meant to help people visualize how the various standards that make up what we think of as Semantic Technology are related to each other. The most recent version (in the footnote) still contains research areas that didn't become standards (user interface, unifying logic, trust and crypto), some that were developed but not widely used (RIF), and some that were developed differently (Trust became PROV-O). There are also many important W3C standards not in that picture.

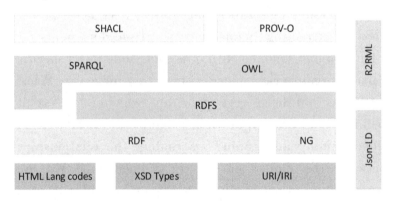

---

[44] https://bit.ly/2Us76gP.

This version includes the standards that most practitioners are following. Most of these have been mentioned above. NG stands for "Named Graph," which is a standard for tagging triples in a triple store, which turns out to be very handy for implementing provenance (PROV-O).

CHAPTER SUMMARY

Building a Data-Centric enterprise has always been a good idea, even if it has not been a widely held good idea. But for most of the time we've been implementing systems, the infrastructure and support did not exist to make it economically feasible. This has changed. Most of the concepts and practices outlined in this section are now more than a decade old. There are standards, tools, and trained professionals that can apply these concepts. We have existence proof. All that remains is creating a plan, putting the pieces together, and getting started.

As we saw in our earlier case studies, it is possible to become Data-Centric without relying on semantic and graph technology, but it demands far more discipline. Linked Data, Knowledge Graphs and Semantic Technology offer capabilities that make it easier to adopt the Data-Centric approach.

The next chapter explores what a few trailblazing companies have done to apply Semantic Technology in a way that is consistent with the theme of this book, which is to enable a Data-Centric enterprise.

CHAPTER 10
Case Studies with Semantic Technology

Before we move on to explore additional facets of the Data-Centric revolution, we'll take this opportunity to present a few more case studies. These examples will help clarify and illuminate the important relationship between Semantic Technology and Data-Centric systems.

GARLIK

According to Steve Harris, Garlik was Data-Centric from Day Zero. From the get-go, they employed a single, simple, shared model of all their data. Garlik, a UK-based startup, was founded in 2005 to provide services to protect consumers from identity theft and fraud.

Steve was the CTO of Garlik from early days to its ultimate sale to Experian. Because of this consistency, Garlik was one of the few companies that had no legacy systems to deal with. Unlike the rest of the case studies here, this means they really had no "negative inertia" or status quo to overcome.

I asked Steve how he had found his clarity and certainty regarding the Data-Centric approach. Prior to Garlik, Steve had been a researcher at the University of Southampton. During his ten years there he developed two insights that have served him well.

The first came from his work on research projects. He observed that there are two primary approaches to building the analytics needed to support a research project: start with the analytics needed and develop the dataset needed to support it versus starting with a fundamental model of the research domain. What he discovered was that while the initial effort was comparable in both approaches, only the latter approach withstood the inevitable changes that come mid-project.

The second insight followed the first, when he came across the semantic web and was convinced of the role it could play in enabling the Data-Centric approach.

In 2005, the opportunity to apply these insights into a commercial venture presented itself. They were funded and their initial project concept was a Business to Consumer (B2C) product focusing on identity theft protection, called Data Patrol, which allowed people to subscribe to a service that would detect whether any of their personal data was compromised or otherwise available anywhere on the web, including the dark web and other sites known for trafficking in stolen identity data.

Around this time, I attended a presentation by Steve's boss, the founding CEO of Garlik, Tom Ilube. Tom had previously been the CIO of Egg, one of the early online banks in the UK. In that capacity, he learned a great deal about how traditional IT systems work. Tom had a very interesting observation on the efficacy of the using Semantic Technology to implement a Data-Centric approach, which was captured in a Q&A session at the Semantic Technology Conference May 20-24, 2007.

> *What we're finding at the moment, in terms of today's benefit, is that it is enabling us to harvest and extract information in a very focused way. So, if we understand more about the semantics of what we are interested in, we can focus our effort more on what we harvest in a much tighter way than we otherwise would have been able to. Having these explicit and flexible models I believe—I have to do a little bit more work on this, but I do know—that it is absolutely true, when I was running the technology in the banking environment [Egg], every time anyone came along and said we want to add a new field, or add any new data to our databases, it was a huge issue, it was*

a huge conversation. The database crew would all get together and put it off six months because no one wanted to mess with their databases, because if you did mess with your databases all your applications got screwed up and all the rest of it. So, it was a really big 'leave this alone.' Where in this environment, where I am now [Garlik] we're sort of hungry for new information sources when we find some new information source, we figure out how to extract the information we're interested in, and we throw it at our 'smushing' bit of the architecture, that puts it into the database and we're away. It just doesn't seem to be anything like the issue that it was in the relational database environment.

Tom Ilube, CEO, Garlik

In the early days of Garlik, triple stores were still in their infancy. So, in addition to building their application, the Garlik team took on the additional task of building their own standards compliant triple store, "4store", followed by "5store" (the inside joke is that all triple stores are built around a tuple of at least 4 parts: subject, predicate, object, and named graph). 4Store was one of the first triple stores to cross the billion-triple threshold, and 5store routinely processed tens of billions of triples in support of the Data Patrol product.

Playing into Steve's observation that the Data-Centric approach really comes into its own in times of change, Garlik found that offering subscriptions direct to consumers for this type of service was pretty much a non-starter. They shifted to a B2B2C model and focused on anti-fraud, rather than identity theft, where their primary customers were banks and other financial institutions. The banks in turn offered this as a service to their customers.

This was a classic pivot for a young lean company. Huge parts of the application had to be changed, to integrate with each of the bank's systems, to present a different look and feel, processes new classes of data, and to adopt the equivalent of a multi-tenant environment. Again, the Data-Centric approach was up to the task.

Garlik was a major supplier of privacy management to the banking industry, when, on December 23, 2011, Garlik was acquired by Experian, the consumer credit company. Those of us involved with Semantic Technology thought this was a way for Experian to get a foothold in this emerging technology and approach.

It seems, however, that gaining a foothold was not the primary motivation. While Experian have kept the Data Patrol product and architecture and offer it to their clients through an API, apparently, the acquisition was more about acquiring Garlik's customer base than about making their thousands of systems Data-Centric. While Experian were at first incredulous about the claims of being able to on board new data sources in days versus months, their sheer size seemed to prevent them from embracing the approach.

This is regrettable but understandable. As reported in Software Wasteland, most large companies have thousands of applications and have established practices, policies, and culture for dealing with the applications, despite their diseconomy. At the time of the acquisition Experian was 500 times larger than Garlik and it was highly unlikely that the tail would wag the dog.

After the acquisition, Steve left Experian and founded another startup, Aistemos. While Aistemos is in a very different business, and has a different technology stack, Steve is testament to the old adage, "A mind, once expanded by a new idea, never returns to its original dimensions" (attributed to Oliver Wendell Holmes). Steve has taken his conviction for data-centrism with him to his new startup.

MONTEFIORE

The Montefiore Medical Center is a 134-year-old integrated network based in the Bronx, NY. It is a $7 billion-a-year enterprise and one of the 50 largest employers in New York State, consisting of 11 hospitals as well as the Albert Einstein teaching hospital, and treats 3 million patients. Montefiore has a long tradition of technical innovation and advancement. They were one of the first institutions to adopt an Electronic Medical Record (in the 1980s) and are leaders in applying patient centered outcomes to their medical interventions.

HISTORY

The Data-Centric system at Montefiore, which is currently called Patient-centered Analytic Learning Machine (PALM), had its roots in a research laboratory in University of Texas Health Science Center at Houston. The central character in this story is Dr. Parsa Mirhaji, what you could call a "triple threat": MD, PhD, and ontologist. In 2009, Dr. Mirhaji established a research laboratory funded by the "Telemedicine Advanced Research and Technology Center-TATRC," whose mission was to bring Semantic Technology to the field of medicine. In his tenure there, Dr. Mirhaji built ontologies and a semantic architecture for large scale health data fusion and integration. They built several point solutions for various medical and population health applications, demonstrating power of semantics in disaster preparedness (during hurricane Katrina), critical care (e.g., major trauma and transfusions), and clinical research. They received three patents[45] and developed considerable intellectual property.

Dr. Mirhaji moved to New York and took on the position of Director, Center for Health Data Innovations at Montefiore. In parallel to running the Informatics practice he took on the construction of a strategic information management plan for Montefiore. One of the tenets of the plan was the central role of data and the need for its integration and management as an enterprise

---

[45] US Patents 8,429,179 8,433,715 and 9,542,647.

asset. The information plan laid the foundation for governance, architecture, competency, and a methodology to evaluate and measure the maturity of the information management at Montefiore. One of the strategic aspects of the plan was to prioritize incremental and iterative progress (agile development) over large 'bet the farm' implementations. The plan also suggested and encouraged leveraging alternate funding sources and early and multi-stakeholder engagement, wherever possible.

One such opportunity presented itself in 2014 when the Patient Centered Outcomes Research Institute (PCORI) went out to bid on a system that could consolidate, integrate, and aggregate patient data from all the major New York City health care providers. The project would be a great proving ground for many of the principles articulated in the strategic plan. It had to be implemented rapidly (there was an 18-month window). There were considerable volumes: 6 major medical centers, 20 million patient records, and 300 million encounters. It stressed the competition that exists between health care providing institutions (they need to cooperate to deliver coordinated care, but they are competing for the limited pool of resources and funds).

The project was a big success. It turned out to be a great learning lab for such inter-organizational governance issues as how to share information without violating privacy and inter-organizational strategic sensitivity. In the processing of the 20 million patient records it was determined that there were 10 million duplicates. This is perhaps not as odd as it first sounds given the proximity of the 6 health centers. A patient matching and deduplication algorithm needed to be built across the entire datascape.

The success of this project encouraged senior management to invest further in internal capabilities. Intel became interested in the project and provided material and engineering support. The PCORI project was executed with traditional and relational technology, as the other health centers had not yet embraced Semantic Technology or graph databases. Internally and in parallel, Parsa's team was building out their own semantic database.

First, they unified medical knowledge (no small feat). There are hundreds of sources of medical knowledge, many of them freely available. Unfortunately, each has its own coding system:

- ICD9 (now ICD10) codifies diseases.

- CPT codes codifies medical procedures.

- MeSH provides a thesaurus style interface to published medical reports and articles.

- LOINC provides standardized nomenclature for tests and findings.

- SNOMED cross references many of these with anatomy and rich relationships between many of the nomenclature systems.

At this point, Montefiore became "knowledge-centric." They had one of the most complete and cross-referenced bodies of knowledge extant. The accumulating knowledge base made it possible to begin bidding on grants that would be difficult or impossible without the pre-organized body of knowledge. These grants are extremely competitive and have very strenuous performance criteria. They bid on and won a key grant to predict respiratory failure and the need for prolonged intubation. Intubation is the process of inserting a breathing tube through the mouth in order to maintain an open airway, for a prolonged period (over 48 hours). It is an expensive and dangerous procedure, uncomfortable for the patient, and often involves complication. It also often saves patients' lives.

The ability to more accurately determine if prolonged intubation is necessary is crucial. The earlier and more accurately it can be predicted, the more time clinicians have to prepare for it or to prevent it.

Combining their medical knowledge with excerpts from their patient database gave Montefiore the table stakes to receive an award to build a real-time analytic system to predict respiratory failure and prolonged intubation, up to 48 hours in advance, and to provide clinicians with a patient-specific checklist of actions and orders that would improve the outcomes and both patient and clinician experience. The analytic system has been built entirely on principles of semantic data integration and interpretation and has been live across Montefiore Medical Center hospitals since January 2017.

They have recently added a sepsis early recognition model. Sepsis in this context is the development of internal infection, usually as byproduct of medical procedures and hospitalization. It is a leading cause of iatrogenic death. In addition to saving lives (generally a good thing), the sepsis module is saving resources. Prior to the building of the sepsis model, Montefiore had 18 people dedicated to Sepsis reporting (there are strict and exhaustive regulatory requirements on sepsis reporting, from many agencies including CMS and NY State Department of Health). Despite the number of people involved (and perhaps because of the number of people involved), the sepsis reporting runs an average of 9 months behind. Much of the delay is in the back and forth between the hospital and the regulators on irregularities or discrepancies in the reported information.

After the implementation of the new sepsis model, which is now near real-time, Montefiore got a letter from the State Department of Health to inform them that for the first time since the inception of their program, the reports had 0 discrepancies. Many of the 18 people working on sepsis reporting have been redeployed to other projects.

CURRENT AND FUTURE INITIATIVES

Montefiore has now converted all the records for all their patients' lives into the system, which was once called the Semantic Data Lake but is now known as Patient-centered Analytic Learning Machine (PALM).

The PALM system is bumping near real-time patient data against their medical knowledge database and looking for anomalous conditions that might be getting overlooked. When a pattern is recognized, an alert is sent to their EMR system. As with all other healthcare institutions, providers experience alert overload, so PALM is trying to be judicious and smart with the signaling. Currently, they are alerting and tracking with the intention, over time, to learn and discover which alerts are acted on or ignored, and which provide the greatest improvement in patient outcomes or provider acceptance. This incremental and automated learning is another feature of PALM.

The Montefiore team is starting to move into their next phase, which will move the system from an analytic only platform to one that includes active participation in the care delivery process. Some of the initial use cases include managing patient flow through the emergency department, managing out-patient appointments, and scheduling. It also works on anticipating patient admission triaging (and staffing accordingly), preventing readmission, automated review of billing claims, fraud detection, and more complex clinical applications that require the fusion of different modalities of data (images

+ free text + structured EMR data) for learning and inferencing.

As I mention in <u>Software Wasteland</u>, sometimes the world serves up "natural experiments" that are the closest thing we get in politics, business, and social systems to the controlled experiments of the hard sciences. In this case, the natural experiment was Montefiore's efforts versus an effort undertaken at MD Anderson.

Montefiore's project has averaged a team of six over five years. They were supplemented with consultants and engineering help from Franz. It seems unlikely to me that the total cost over the five years was over $10 million. More interestingly, the net cost was far less when you consider the grants that were used to fund much of the work, as well as in-kind investments into the endeavor by Franz, Cisco and Intel.

MD Anderson launched the much publicized, "Watson goes to Medical School." Like Medical School for humans, this was not inexpensive. The total tab for Watson's matriculation was $62 million. Apparently, Watson flunked out of medical school as the project was cancelled with nothing implemented.

We don't know whether the MD Anderson project attempted a Data-Centric approach and failed. We do know that Montefiore adopted a hybrid "Data-Centric plus incremental" approach. Montefiore underspent MD Andersen at least by a factor of ten. They out delivered by an even greater margin, as by my assessment, they achieved much of what MD Anderson set out to do and have an implemented system to show for it.

CHAPTER SUMMARY

These case studies, coupled with many more that we are familiar with but were not able to get permission to publish, tell us several things. The first is an existence proof: it is possible to build a Data-Centric enterprise with Semantic Technology.

The second thing these case studies teach us is that leaning into Semantic Technology can help the mental transition that is needed to embrace radical simplicity.

These case studies also demonstrated how semantics and graph databases make the evolution of data structures simple and seamless.

CHAPTER 11
Application Software is the Problem

The previous section showcased firms that are reaping great gains from their Data-Centric initiatives. One aspect of their success that we only touched on in the case studies, and which we will elaborate on now, is the massive reduction in their code base. In this chapter, we will examine more closely the four ways that Data-Centric methods lead to massive reduction in code bloat. But before we get to the "how," we must address the "why." When you start thinking about reducing your code, you may find yourself asking the following questions:

- Isn't software a good thing? Why would we want to reduce the amount of application software that we have?

- How much application software do we have? How much do we want?

- If most of our application code is unnecessary, where does it all come from?

Pointing out that most application software is unnecessary will make a lot of people uncomfortable. There are millions of application developers and application maintainers who have built their careers around coding software. There are hundreds of thousands of executives who have been investing in application implementation projects. There is an established $400 billion System Integration industry and another $400 billion Application Software industry.

The players in these arenas will probably not be thrilled at the idea that their efforts have been largely inefficient and misdirected. Unfortunately, though, we must face and accept this hard truth.

ISN'T SOFTWARE A GOOD THING?

Of course software is a good thing. We couldn't have traveled to the Moon without it, and it brings us the wonders of the internet (and its kitten videos). Even enterprises have benefited from their investments in inventory control systems and customer relationship management systems.

However, there are many ways in which software is also a liability. As we examine several of these drawbacks, you'll see how they can quickly stack upon each other, ultimately tipping the scales deep into liability for most companies. We will explore techniques that will allow us to keep the value of our applications while shedding most of the liability.

IS APPLICATION CODE AN ASSET?

The current application-centric view of technology naturally considers application code to be an asset. After all, it took million lines of complex application code in order to automate and streamline our existing processes. Because this code has played such a vital role in the past, it is difficult for many people to change their view and see it as a liability.

The sheer volume and complexity of code eats up most of the support costs in IT. We have seen large projects justified by the large number of complex applications that must be integrated to solve a problem. Until we can see clearly that this isn't necessary, and indeed is a detriment, it is easy to be taken in by this line of reasoning.

When you implement an application system, you incur a one-time capital expense (the often very expensive cost

of a new application implementation project) and three
ongoing liabilities:

1. You must maintain the integration of this
    application with, potentially, all other
    applications in your firm.

2. You must maintain the code base, correcting
    defects as they arise and modifying it to meet
    changes in the environment. You may incur this
    cost yourself or you may pay a vendor to do this,
    but the cost is incurred.

3. Each new system increases the cognitive load of
    the people who are to use it. The more systems,
    and the more complex they are, the higher this
    cognitive load.

You also incur the operating costs of running the system
(the hardware, services, and networking costs). While
reducing code bloat will generally also reduce operating
costs, the effect is not nearly as linear.

The first two liabilities make up most of the IT budget of
enterprises. The developers are either maintaining
existing code, writing new code (making the problem
worse as we'll see), or maintain the integration between
systems.

The third liability is mostly felt in the lines of business,
where staff spends additional time learning more systems
and using multiple systems to get a task accomplished.

The third liability also drives a great deal of the cost of internal help desks.

These liabilities are the gifts that keep on taking. Once you have installed an application system, the obligation is to maintain it and continue until it is decommissioned.

HOW MUCH CODE DO WE HAVE?

There is a micro answer to this (at the firm level) and a macro answer (the total economy).

The micro answer varies a great deal from firm to firm. But if you are a $5 billion a year firm or agency, you will have thousands of application systems. Each has its own data model, which has thousands of concepts. You easily have 1 million concepts, and the upper limit (as discussed in the second section) is 1 billion concepts.

The industry average is to have 1,300 lines of code per every concept in the schema of your databases. It is therefore highly likely that you have 1.3 billion lines of code under management.

What is surprising is how much of this code is functionally doing the same thing, but it can't be reused either because it was written to a different data model, or it was written in a language that makes it hard to reuse. In the next section, we will attempt to estimate how much code you would need if you built for reuse.

The difference is staggering, and it is in line with what we have seen in these case studies.

The other way of looking at this is from the macro point of view: how much unique software code there is in the world? It's a bit hard to nail this down because most estimates are overcounting because of the many nearly cost-free copies of code that exist.

Perhaps the best way to back into an upper limit for the amount of code that exists in the world is to reflect on the cost of producing it. Code is mostly written by hand. Unfortunately, there is still very little automated code generation going on.

Currently, most software code is written by hand, at a cost between $10 and $100 per line of tested code in production. If you take the high end of software development professional services expenditures at $1 trillion and the most optimistic estimate for productivity, we get an upper limit of 100 billion lines of code being produced per year.

Many IT professionals do not write code at all. 100 billion lines per year seems a bit high. Looking a bit deeper, I found these estimates:

- 111 billion lines per year—a curiously precise number but attempts to drill down into the supporting detail came up empty-handed.[46]

- 250 billion lines of code for the installed base of COBOL[47]—given it has been around for 50 years, this would suggest they have been adding to it at the rate of 5 billion lines per year. I'm pretty sure these numbers include many copies of programs including packages and libraries.

- 100 million "pull requests"[48]—github, which is the most popular code repository, reported that they had hit their 100 millionth posting of code. Most posts contain more than a handful of lines of code (although there is a lot of copying going on). If the average net addition for a pull request is 100 lines, then we are at 10 billion (and this is likely less than half of all active code).

Let's say we've been adding a billion lines of code to the installed base every year for the last several decades, which seems reasonable, we have a large legacy to deal with.

As mentioned above, the COBOL industry is believed to have 250 billion lines of installed code.

---

[46] https://bit.ly/2KQ5EFM.

[47] https://bit.ly/2VVMwab.

[48] https://bit.ly/2ceSeQb.

Whether tens of billions or hundreds of billions, we collectively have a lot of application software, and even at hundreds of millions to billions, each firm has a great deal of that under management.

SOFTWARE IS EATING THE WORLD

Marc Andreessen, co-founder of Netscape and partner in the VC firm, Andreessen Horowitz, wrote a memorable article called, "Why Software is Eating the World,"[49] in which he correctly points out that the value add in category after category of companies is shifting from bricks to bits. Amazon, the world's largest retailer, is essentially a software company.

But Marc is overlooking the dark side of software eating the world. For the typical enterprise, the creation and maintenance of software are eating their resources. Most firms (except software companies, interestingly) are incurring more costs maintaining their software systems than they are generating in profits.

Maintaining application software that is marginally useful, and at the same time is consuming resources at a prodigious rate, is a major drag on most enterprises.

---

[49] https://bit.ly/2vTAYYp.

HOW MUCH DO WE NEED?

Visual Studio is one of the single largest pieces of software in the world. It's over 55 million lines of code. And one of the things that I found out in this study is more than 98 percent of it is completely irrelevant.[50]

Chris Granger

Windows 10 has 50 million lines of code. The Linux operating system is 15 million lines of code. An incredibly high percentage of both are consumed with backward compatibility. The Chromebook OS is about 5 million lines of code. It is not hard to conceive of operating systems using far, far less. But let's accept 10 million as a reasonable number for an operating system.

Let's accept tens of millions of lines for each database and piece of middleware we need (do we need dozens or hundreds?).

Finally, the real question is: how much application software code does the world need? QuickBooks is 10 million lines of code. Estimates on the size of the SAP (the dominant enterprise software vendor) range from 40 million to 400 million. There are thousands and thousands of enterprise application systems.

---

[50] As reported in https://bit.ly/2hxnMlQ.

If an operating system didn't need to backwardly support our vast legacy systems, then it would need far less than 1 million lines of code. The same goes for any piece of middleware. And far, far less for any given application.

As I was putting this chapter together, I thought I would check whether these statistics mirrored recent developments. In the chapter on enabling technology, I mentioned a new type of data store called a 'graph database' or a 'triple store.' These databases play an analogous role to the relational DBMS's such as Oracle and Microsoft SQL. I asked the CEO of one of the triple store vendors how many lines of code were in their offering. After conferring with the technology team, he reported that their server, which supports a surprisingly high number of features and interfaces, was implemented in 250,000 lines of code. Another 150,000 lines of code are for regression and systems testing. This is 1% the size of most commercial Relational Databases and, I think, is indicative of the order of magnitude of improvement that is possible.

I have personal experience with leading teams to build, from scratch, complex ERP systems. In each case, the functionality was more complex than leading ERP vendor offerings. But unlike the tens of millions of lines of code in a packaged ERP system, our systems were built with precursors to the approaches we will discuss in the next chapter. In each case, most of the application code was generated (the total amount of code in each system was in the order of 5 million lines), but the number of lines that were custom written was under 100,000. As a result, the cost to build the system in addition to implementation in each case was under $3 million, which would be a fraction of the cost of a packaged implementation for the same functionality.

The world has many billions of lines of software code currently. We need several million. We probably have 1000 times more than we need. Someone paid to have this all built. That is a sunk cost. Even as I write, more software of marginal net value is being introduced.

But the real tax is the liability of using all this software. As we said earlier, the cost of maintaining, integrating, and learning this code is the real ongoing cost.

It's sort of like cleaning out your attic. You may realize that, in principle, you need almost none of what you have in your attic, but you are unlikely to do anything until you move. Even then there is a pretty good chance you will pack up most of that crap and put it in your new attic.

> *I'm not sure that programming has to exist at all. Or at least software developers.*[51]

> Bret Victor

---

[51] https://bit.ly/2hxnMlQ.

Application software is just the same. Unlike the junk in your attic, though, this application software bloat is costing you a great deal of money on an ongoing basis.

WHERE DOES IT ALL COME FROM?

If we have a lot of unnecessary software, it behooves us to ask: where did it come from, and why does it persist?

This is a deep question, with many facets, some of which I touched on in Software Wasteland. Let me summarize from there and elaborate a bit more.

I believe there are three major contributors:

1. The relationship of code to schema
2. Perverse incentives
3. How software developers think.

THE RELATIONSHIP OF CODE TO SCHEMA

As I mentioned earlier, in a traditional application system, the code and the database schema are bound in a very unhelpful way. The code is written to the schema. If there is a Customer Table, Orders Table, and a Products Table, the code will access the customer table, pick up a few attributes (perhaps create an order header), and write out the date, customer ship to, and bill to address. Order lines will be written by accessing the product tables and getting on hand availability, prices, and descriptions.

Ah, if it were only that simple. And if it were only done once and done consistently. But there are dozens to hundreds of systems with customer data. Each structured differently. Each table and field have a different name. The level of abstraction might be different. The tables might be in different brands of databases. This means that the code written for one application is not usable for the other. There is virtually no reuse at the business concept level across applications, despite huge potential benefit for doing so.

Why didn't everyone write to a single shared schema? That was what ERP was meant to be, but the technology at the time meant that a single shared schema would have to be massively complex to handle even a portion of the needs of a large enterprise.

The technology now exists to implement a single, simple, shared, extensible model, but habits die hard.

PERVERSE INCENTIVES

A great deal of the IT industry benefits from writing and maintaining large bodies of code.

One of the strategies that many systems implementers and systems integrators employ at the start of a project is to bring in as much software as they can. There is a belief that the problems of the implementation can be solved at a categorical level. That is, just list all the aspects of the problem that need to be solved. Let's say you need some content management functionality, and some search engine optimization functionality, and some multilingual functionality, and some messaging capability, and some task management functionality. You acquire one of each of these and start your project. This has become far easier in the age of open source as there is always an open source project you might use.

This creates the illusion of progress, while at the same time making the project bigger, and therefore putting you behind schedule. The reason these acquisitions make the project bigger is each has its own level of complexity. Each piece of the puzzle must be mastered. Several people will be assigned to each technology and will be consumed with mastering it. Each piece of the puzzle has its own shortcomings and its own latent defects. These take time to uncover, but they are there.

The real complexity, and therefore, the added cost, lies in getting all these disparate pieces to interact. They were designed independently and making them interact takes a great deal of effort.

By the time it dawns on the sponsors of the project that things are ballooning out of control, it's usually too late to go back. When you realize that it is spiraling out of control, statistically you would be better off admitting defeat and canceling the project. However, we know from a host of studies that people are reluctant to abandon their "investments" and fail to treat them as the sunk costs that they are.

The real question, which I don't have an answer for, is: "Is this an intentional strategy that system implementers employ, or do they sincerely believe that loading up on software at the beginning of a project will be beneficial?" It almost doesn't matter, as the result is the same, but I'd be curious. Most of the small number of systems integrators that I know, seem to sincerely think that this is an inherently complex thing to do, and that adding more complex software to their project is helping.

HOW PROGRAMMERS THINK, AND WHY THIS IS A BUSINESS PROBLEM

What follows are some generalizations. Some programmers are thoughtful designers. But most aren't.

Programmers are problem solvers. At least, the good ones are. However, they tend to solve the problem at hand and care very little about the overall impact on the firm.

Additionally, programmers care far more about the structure of the data they are dealing with and much less about its meaning. Programmers like to solve problems with code. When a business analyst tells them about an exception, they tend to write an "if statement" to handle the exception. Their assessment is that solving a problem this way is more expedient. It is. But it misses all sorts of opportunity to solve problems in ways that non-programmers could maintain (through table-driven or parametric approaches), and it tends to create point solutions rather than study a family of problems and solve them as one.

We worked with a multilevel-marketing client (who shall remain nameless) who retained a firm to build them a custom online system. There are some complexities to multilevel marketing, especially in the area of what they call "genealogy" or the management of the relationships that lead to the building of their referrals tree. There is some very complex logic in calculating the upstream and downstream commission sharing. The rest of the site is just generic product sales.

We weren't quite prepared for what we saw. The system had 2,500 tables. What made for a very curious coincidence is that they offered 2,500 products for sale. This really was just a coincidence, each product did not have its own table, but I've been fascinated ever since as to how anyone could possibly design a system like that. Earlier, we discussed a client that worked with 1,000,000 complex electrical parts. Their existing system had 700 tables, but the new system we designed had only 46. Clearly, there is no relation between the number of tables in a schema and the number of parts in a warehouse.

We would expect this multilevel marketing system to require about 100 concepts (total of classes plus properties) to handle much more complex product catalogs and online point of sale. We know, because we prepared a design for their genealogy system, that the genealogy portion of the system would also add far less than 100 new concepts to the model. We didn't count the number of columns in the existing systems, but our observation is that most relational systems average more than 10 columns per table, so it seems reasonable to guess that this system has over 27,500 concepts that must be programmed to (2,500 tables plus 25,000 columns). This system is approximately 100 times more complex than it needs to be. This happens all the time. There was clearly very little thought put into the design of this system, just lots of coding, reacting, and adding more code to solve the next request.

A system that is 100 times as complex as it needs to be, 100 times more expensive to build, and 100 times more expensive to implement has 100 times as many latent defects and will cost 100 times as much to maintain.

CHAPTER SUMMARY

It seems like application software is a good thing. Certainly, the first application systems built were great boons. In the 1950s, a company that automated its payroll system had an advantage over one that didn't. This led us to believe that we needed application code to build all the user interfaces and codify all the rules that we need to automate our business processes.

But application software (really all software) is a liability as much as it is an asset. The complexity of the software is what makes the liability. As systems become more complex, they become more of a liability. They are a liability because of the latent defects that the code harbors and which come out to cause problems at very inopportune times. The complexity of application software exhibits liability characteristics when we try to change it. The complexity of application software is what makes change difficult.

The good news is that it is now possible to build most of most application systems without application code. After decades of staring at application systems, people have finally begun treating applications as if they were a business domain. The result, as we'll see in the next chapter, is what is often called "model-driven development," or the "low-code / no-code" movement.

CHAPTER 12
Data-Centric Means
Massive Code Reduction

To summarize the previous chapter as briefly and succinctly as possible: we have more code than we need. A lot more.

The typical enterprise application has over 1 million lines of application source code. Many have tens of millions of lines. Some have hundreds of millions. Even if you purchased the code, the complexity of all those lines of code leaks out all over the place. There are weird bugs caused by odd combinations of behaviors in different parts of the system. Things interact in ways that are hard to predict. There are myriad latent bugs in the code that rear their heads at the worst possible time.

Luckily, adopting a Data-Centric approach can contribute to a wholesale reduction in code, lowering the liability of that code without reducing its value. This is achieved through five mechanisms:

1. Reducing schema complexity
2. Reducing schema variety
3. Making possible massive reuse
4. Writing to a subset of the schema
5. Replacing code with data.

REDUCING SCHEMA COMPLEXITY

The single biggest improvement brought about by enlightened use of semantics is to dramatically simplify our data models. As we saw in the Standard & Poors, Market Intelligence case study, it is possible to build a Data-Centric enterprise with a traditional and complex data model. In the case of Market Intelligence there are over 8,000 classes in their model. Adding semantics to the solution can drastically reduce the complexity of the model at the center of a Data-Centic approach. As we described earlier, a model built using Semantic Technology is called an Ontology. An Ontology designed to cover most of the information in an enterprise is called an "Enterprise Ontology." An Enterprise Ontology is the preferred center to a Data-Centric Architecture. In our experience a semantically driven Data-Centric model (and Enterprise Ontology) can cover an enterprises' key concepts with a few hundred classes. This simplification does not come for free. It takes intention and discipline, but it is possible.

We know of many ontologies that are not simple. SNOMED (the ontology of Diseases and Symptoms) has over 300,000 classes. It is hard to know what the "important" ones are when there are that many. It is also hard to know which ones are safe to code to as they are less likely to change. The Montefiore ontology that we reported on above has a few dozen classes, which is interesting considering that they imported the whole of SNOMED. What they did differently was model the few key concepts in SNOMED (Disease, Symptom, Finding, Contraindication, and the like) as classes, and then treated the remaining 300,000 + as instances of these classes. This reduces schema complexity and reduces the temptation of developers to code to the schema.

REDUCING SCHEMA VARIETY

Up until now, we have mostly been talking about schema complexity, that is, the sheer number of items that are in a schema or a set of schemas. When one implements an application that mostly overlaps the domain coverage of an existing application, let's say you implement another inventory management application, (this happens all the time) you have increased the schema complexity of the whole (if this were your only two applications you would have doubled your enterprise schema complexity).

The impact of this increased complexity can either be heightened or diminished depending on the variety between the schemas. If the terms are similar in the two applications and the structures are comparable, the added complexity is far easier to manage. If however, the two systems use different terms and structure the data differently, this variety will add to the already increased complexity.

If we look at where data models come from, we understand why they are as varied as they are. Data models and the schemas derived from them are completely made up. Data modelers interview users and adopt the terms they use. They are highly subject to whomever they talk to first, as these first few bits of the model form a sort of "seed" that the rest of the model grows around.

By way of a representative example, we worked with a $1 billion-a-year Worker's Compensation Insurance firm that implemented receivables functionality in 23 different systems — each of which had a completely unique way to express the concepts surrounding the receivable. They hadn't intended to do this, it just happened in the course of business, as it does in all businesses.

This firm had many safety-related goals, all of which supported an overall mission to provide a "safety net" for injured workers. The firm provided the inspection certificates in elevators. These certificates cost money. If the landlord doesn't pay for the certificate at the time of inspection (most don't), there is a liability created, which is a receivable for the agency. In their data schema, they had terms such as "Elevator Certificate," "Landlord," and "Conveyance" (i.e., the generic terms for elevators, escalators, and cranes).

A receivable in the Worker's Compensation part of the business might be for "Claims Overpayment," which usually arises when an injured worker has been receiving benefit checks and goes back to work before notifying the agency. A "Claims Overpayment" liability (and therefore receivable to the company) is described in terms of the "Claim" and the "Worker." The Elevator Permit System and the Claims Overpayment System were each creating "receivables" and yet neither used that term or any other term in common. Even the amount of the receivable is "Certificate Fee" in the Elevator Permit system and "Claim overpayment balance" in the Claims Overpayment System.

As mentioned this didn't just happen twice, there were 23 different systems that had Accounts Receivable functionality, and therefore had a portion of their schema devoted to this, despite the fact that each of them used completely different terms and structures to represent the receivables.

We can address this issue by converging on a shared model. We start by recognizing that liability is a bilateral obligation. That is, the party making the obligation commits with another party on the other side of the commitment. An obligation to pay money results in the right to receive payment (the "receivable"). This is true for all variations of receivables. We now merely need to align the specifics with the general case. In the case of the elevator permit, the landlord is the obligor. For claims overpayment the injured worker is the obligor. The evidence for the obligation is the certificate for the elevator and the claim payments for the worker. Once aligned, getting a firm-wide view of receivables (and as a bonus, revenue recognition) is just a matter of querying on the shared concepts.

MAKING POSSIBLE MASSIVE REUSE

Code reuse was a major mantra at one point, and it has some appeal. We know that most code we write has already been written before, hundreds if not thousands of times over. And yet, it is devilishly hard to reuse it. One reason for the difficulty is that each of the many times the code is rewritten, it's in a particular programming language for a particular position in a deployment stack.

Object-oriented programming was originally mooted as a way of organizing for reuse. Coupling behavior with data structures, and then extending these data structures, could lead to code reuse. But this rarely worked at the scale it needed to. It worked within individual applications but rarely across applications.

Another approach gaining traction (but that needs to align with Semantic Technology to fulfill its promise) is microservices.

A MICROSERVICES ARCHITECTURE WITH MASSIVE REUSE

A Microservices Architecture is one where small units of functionality are reused throughout a major system. When well implemented, microservices achieve what object-oriented intended to but rarely did. What prevented object-oriented design from achieving its potential was that in almost all implementations, it achieved reuse through inclusion and compilation into massive monoliths of code.

Microservices are not compiled in or bound into runtime monoliths. This gives them the potential to provide very generalized functions.

Imagine if we had a Customer Relationship Management system (CRM, which is primarily a sales management system), and we wanted to alert the sales manager if a major deal was in danger. The application programming approach would be to add some code to detect the criteria (let's say the salesperson reduces the likelihood of closing a deal by more than 20%) and sends the salesperson's manager an email. This will work, but we now have a very specific set of conditions marbled into our CRM code.

A micro-services approach might involve building a couple of general-purpose services. Say there was a monitoring service and a notification service. Each is very general and needs to be qualified with parameters, but these parameters can be a) application specific and b) expressed in data. By changing most of the specifics of the logic from code to data, we move to a system that is far simpler to maintain and evolve.

The parameters for the monitor function might say, "When sales.opportunity.likelihood reduces by > 20% send message A24 to sales.opportuity.salesManager." The same notification service might also be testing for inventory levels dropping below reorder points or estimated task completion date exceeding planned date by more than 14 days.

Likewise, a notification service receives the result of the monitoring function. The service uses this information to determine whom to notify and how (with an email, an SMS, or an item on a "to do" list).

It is our belief that a well-executed architecture contains a tiny fraction of the code found in traditional application-centric environments.

WRITING TO A SUBSET OF THE SCHEMA

A traditional application system has a "flat" datascape. That is, all tables are more or less equal. As more tables are added to the application, additional code must be written to deal with them.

Object-oriented development initiated a style of development where, with well-designed object-oriented systems, much of the work could be done writing to high-level abstract classes and the differences coded to the more specific sub-classes. For instance, an object-oriented mortgage system might code most of their logic to an abstract representation of a mortgage, and then supply the small variations needed to implement things like the difference between fixed rate and variable rate mortgages (or differences in maximum loan amounts available for single family or multifamily properties).

The Data-Centric approach takes this idea to another level. We are finding that systems can be built with knowledge of two relatively small subsets of a schema: the primitive domain concepts and the schema that represents the metadata for the model-driven portion of the ontology.

We will take up the model-driven portion of the story in more detail in the next section, but the short version is that we can replace 90%+ of application code written against the application schema with a single set of code written against the model schema, in addition to the variations expressed in the model.

With or without a model-driven approach, there is great economy in focusing code on a small number of primitive concepts. There are real differences at the application level between some key concepts. For instance, you only want to place objects with geospatial references on a map, and you only want to put items on a timeline or in a calendar if they have dates associated with them. Normally these types of distinctions are made at the application schema level. Unfortunately, doing so means dealing with the thousands of concepts expressed in the application schema.

While there are real differences in the application data, we are finding there are typically between a dozen and two dozen differences that need to be recognized at the application level. We call these concepts the "primitive" concepts as they are generally not expressed in terms of other objects. In most industries or domains, these include:

- Geospatial entities (points, lines, areas on the surface of the earth)

- Buildings

- Physical Items

- Physical Substances

- Events (and their relationship to time)

- People

- Organizations

- Measurements

- Units of Measure

- Addresses (including communication addresses)

- Obligations (most business systems are primarily about the recognition and liquidation of obligations)

- Goals and Intentions

- Content and Documents.

Some practitioners have come to a very similar set of base primitives in their vocabulary classification. John Gorman's top-level model, Q6,[52] comprises 19 classes organized by the six interrogative or "question" words (who, what, when, why, where, and how).

John Gorman's opinion, and ours as well is that the important differences between application concepts (which is where real behavioral differences are found) can be expressed in a few dozen concepts.

CODE REDUCTION THROUGH INTEGRATION ELIMINATION

One more area where you can find code reduction is through the elimination of integration (or interface) code. In a traditional system, if you have "workers data" in

---

[52] https://bit.ly/2GlgWwa.

one application and "employee data" in another system, sooner or later you write code to extract from one to combine with the other.

This is not a trivial amount of code. Many firms spend 40-60% of their IT budget on the creation and maintenance of this code. By eliminating the need for this code, you eliminate a lot of waste.

There are two mechanisms that contribute to the integration code reduction. One is the rationalization and harmonization of the data models; the other is the mechanism we described in the section on Linked Data. In current technology, connecting data in two different systems relies on some form of deducing that two rows are referring to the same thing (there are often a set attributes that must be compared). Using Linked Data, the equivalent of joining rows is handled by the system, further eliminating code.

CHAPTER SUMMARY

One of the big benefits of a Data-Centric approach is its role in reducing complexity. Reducing complexity, directly and indirectly, reduces the amount of code that needs to be built and maintained.

At the level of individual applications, code and complexity can be reduced by reducing the size of individual application data models. The amount of code needed in a system of systems can be reduced even more by eliminating the need for integration through rationalizing data models between applications. Further improvements come from reducing the subset of the schema to which programmers must code through abstraction or through data hiding in microservices.

The biggest savings are achieved when code quantity is directly reduced by replacing the code with data. The next chapter will focus on all the benefits of adopting model-driven development).

CHAPTER 13
Model-Driven Everything

We have noticed a shift toward model-driven development (and away from application code-driven development) often co-occurs with the shift toward Data-Centric approaches. This isn't surprising if you consider the mindsets and thought patterns behind the two concepts. When someone embarks on a Data-Centric journey, they begin thinking differently about their data. They see different relationships between data and applications, and between data and architecture. This has been evident in the case studies discussed thus far.

MODEL-DRIVEN DEVELOPMENT

The concept of model-driven development has its roots in parametric Computer Aided Design (CAD) and Computer

Aided Software Engineering (CASE) systems. Parametric CAD describes an approach to designing physical parts; the approach is especially productive when designing intermediate parts embedded within a complex manufactured artifact.

When you look at a complex assembled product, such as a car, you might think that all the parts are independently designed and assembled. The average automobile contains over 30,000 parts[53]. Some common parts (e.g., standard screws and bolts) can be used across many different variations in the drive train, but many unique or specialty parts must be modified with each redesign.

One common intermediate part in an automobile is the *motor mount*, which attaches its motor to its frame. The size, shape, and fit of the motor mount piece depends on the motor and the frame; all three must fit together perfectly. As such, if the company decides the following year to extend the chassis by 3 inches or to put in a more powerful (and heavier) motor, last year's motor mount will no longer properly fit when building the new model Historically, this meant that every redesign sent engineers back to a literal drawing board, forcing them to very precisely redesign each intermediate part to the new specifications.

---

[53] https://bit.ly/2ok9mb2.

But that was then, and this is now. Instead of hand-designing every intermediate part, automotive designers have figured out how to build and utilize a digital models of many of the intermediate parts.

The engineers working on our motor mount could construct a digital model of a typical motor mount with relative ease. Within this model the engineers could adjust many input variables, including frame length, motor weight and torque. Based on these new parameters, the model would produce as output a revised design for the motor mount, optimized to perfectly fit the current year's model.

CASE was the software industry's first attempt to emulate such parametric CAD modeling in the 1980s. Early CASE systems were primarily code generation systems. Developers noticed that many software modules were incredibly repetitive. CASE systems allowed the developers to describe the differences and generate the software equivalent of boilerplate.

Early systems were limited in scope (they could only generate simple form-based systems typically) and were often just a way to get a first draft of the application code, but they were a start.

The movement largely went underground through the 1990s as the majority of application implementation was package based, and therefore, model-driven approaches didn't apply. While it was underground, progress continued to be made.

While I was at a healthcare dot com in the 1990s, we designed, built, and patented the first fully model-driven application architecture.[54] Many other variations have emerged since then, to the point that Gartner has now noticed the movement.

LOW-CODE AND NO-CODE

There are now at least a dozen firms with model-driven offerings. Gartner coined the complementary terms "low-code" and "no-code"[55] , and the terms typically appeal to different audiences. "Low-code" systems generate code from the inputs the designer gives it; this approach appeals more to software developers looking for a productivity edge. "No-code" systems build the general functionality once and then supply the variation via input variables. "No-Code" systems tend to appeal to business analysts who wish to deliver business functionality without necessarily ever compiling anything.

Salesforce really popularized the low-code/no-code concept. Some of the leading firms offering either low-code or no-code systems include:

- Salesforce Lightning
- Out Systems

---

[54] US Patent 6,049,673.

[55] https://bit.ly/2ZlupN7.

- EnterpriseWeb
- AppSyngery (from the Sokil case study)
- Appian
- Microsoft Power Apps
- Zoho Creator
- FluidOps
- Mendix

The maturity of the model-driven approach is a great boon to adopters of the Data-Centric approach; more and more of the functionality of the system can be delivered without writing additional code. We have built systems with no application code (and very little architectural code), so we know that this approach can be married with a Data-Centric outlook.

The following sections will offer a high-level glimpse of the possibilities opened by model driven systems. For those interested in how to implement this in an enterprise architecture, look for more detail in this volume's companion book, <u>The Data-Centric Architecture</u>.

DECLARATIVE CODE

We've become quite familiar with declarative queries due to the popularity of relational databases and SQL. The thing that marked the big difference between SQL and its predecessors was that with prior technology, the query or the transversal was intimately tied with how the data was physically stored. A programmer would use their knowledge of the storage structure (e.g., linked lists or hash tables) to optimize data access. The problem was that this knowledge became embedded in the application code. This approach is often called "procedural" because the knowledge of how to access the data is locked up in application code. The "how" is thoroughly enmeshed with the "what."

With "declarative queries," the query writer describes what they want to do, and the query manager (software) works out how to do it. The power here is that the query manager can learn over time. The declarative query need not be rewritten every time the query manager comes up with a more performant way of executing it. It is this aspect that allowed Relational Databases to go from woefully inferior query performance to mostly superior query performance.

In the same way that we can convert queries from procedural to declarative, we can do the same thing with applications. Right now, almost all application code is procedural, and therefore, a great deal of the "how" is mixed in with the "what." The "model" in model-driven development is a declarative description of what the application needs to do independent of how it does it.

An application needs to do a great deal of work; however, almost all of what an application does can be reduced to a model, and therefore, be made declarative.

MODEL-DRIVEN CONSTRAINTS AND VALIDATION

If you study traditional application software, the first depressing thing you realize is that most of the code just shuttles data back and forth from database schema or API (application programming interfaces) to screen fields and forms. We tend to think of the "high value" code in an application system as being the code that captures the sophisticated business logic. The code that just "shuttles" data back and forth between the database, the API, the Object Layer, the browser, and any other intermediary structure is relatively "low value" code. It is necessary, due to the architecture of the system, but it adds very little net business benefit.

After this "shuttling" code, the next most common category of code is that which performs validation and constraint management. Most of this is incredibly trivial. This type of code often checks whether entered data is of the appropriate syntactic type (e.g., numbers, characters, or dates), whether data has the right number of characters (e.g., in 5-digit zip codes), matches a pattern (e.g., the XXX-XX-XXXX pattern of U.S. social security numbers), or matches a predefined list of valid values (e.g., countries, states, or genders).

"Sophisticated" validation includes cross-field validation (is the "from" date before the "to" date), completeness (are all the required fields present), and cardinality (ensuring that each project has at least one and not more than two sponsors).

The sad thing, when you look very long and very hard at a traditional application system, far less than 1% of the code could be considered to be "high value" providing benefit to the business. This "business logic" is typically marbled in amongst the million or more lines of "low value" code, making it hard to find and modify the high-value code.

The good news is that most of the low-value code can be model-driven, using standards such as SHACL from the W3C.

MODEL-DRIVEN CONSTRAINTS

As we mentioned, most of the type of constraints described above are now covered by a W3C specification called SHACL. SHACL stands for the SHApes Constraint Language. SHACL defines "shapes" that portions of the graph must conform to. A shape might declare that a person in a given database repository may have up to two biological parents. This constrains the shape of the graph.

What we didn't mention is that SHACL is a model driven language. The constraints are expressed in data, triple formatted data. A SHACL engine then interprets the shape models and determines if the data conforms before allowing an update to persist to the database.

MODEL-DRIVEN UI

80-90% of the user interfaces in most applications could easily be generated from a model without any application code. There is a need to write or purchase some infrastructure code that can interpret the model, but once this is done, it executes all models without additional code.

Our experience is that there will be a handful of high use and high-value interfaces that you may want to have hand-coded, so rather than shoot for 100%, you should have a more modest ambition. Keep in mind if you do implement 90% of your user interfaces as models, you will have eliminated 90% of your code, 90% of the defects, and 90% of your future maintenance cost.

In order to implement a model-driven user interface, you will need a mechanism to establish use cases. If you have adopted a model-driven constraint approach, this will provide most of the structure you need for the UI generation. You will need to add:

- Grouping (which fields in a form you would like grouped together)

- Sequencing (within a group and between groups, what you would like the order to be)

- Entry or tab sequence (where the cursor goes on entry)

- Default values (what value is supplied if the user doesn't supply anything)

- Actions supported (edit, cancel, delete, as well as any custom actions).

These days most UIs will be web-based, much of the styling and aesthetics will be driven by style sheets, and default designs will use Responsive Web Design (RWD). This means that UI will adapt gracefully for different form factors, such as a cell phone.

MODEL-DRIVEN IDENTITY MANAGEMENT

Identity management concerns assigning unique IDs to items and detecting whether an item has been encountered in the past and therefore, can reuse the previously assigned ID. It also involves detecting whether other systems have assigned different identifiers to the same item and maintaining alias lists.

This can be achieved in a model-driven manner. It is a matter of expressing the identity rules in executable models. We have had clients who refer to this as their "match spec," and we have adopted that term. Some match spec implementations supply confidence factors— how certain are we that these two records represent the same item?

For each class of item, at least one match spec is prepared. At the time of addition or maintenance, the architecture can determine whether the attributes of a given item (e.g., Person, Organization, Product, or Task) match those of a previously captured item. If they do match, their identities can be merged. There are several approaches to implementing the merge, ranging from ID rewriting to keeping lists of aliases.

MODEL-DRIVEN SECURITY

Application security is primarily focused on authorization—what are the rules governing who can see or modify what information? Unfortunately, most existing applications also deal with "authentication," which is determining the identity and credentials of the user accessing the system. The reason I say this is unfortunate is that authentication clearly belongs at the architecture/ infrastructure level. You should be able to log in once and have your credentials forwarded to the various applications you use. Many firms are making progress on this, most call it their "single sign-on" project. The reason it has been so slow to adopt is that many applications were designed to run on a stand-alone basis and integrating with various enterprise authentication schemes was an afterthought.

We will assume that an authentication scheme is in place. Authorization is harder than it first sounds and is very poorly handled now. We believe a model-driven approach to authorization can improve things greatly, and at the same time, make access management simpler and more consistent.

The shortcomings of current authorization schemes are due to the way the application-centric mindset has carved up the problem. Currently, authorization is managed on an application-by-application basis. Each application defines a set of "roles" that determine what people can do. Typically, there is some sort of admin or superuser role that can do almost anything. There are roles for people who can change other roles, a handful of function-specific roles (e.g., Accounts Receivable and Accounts Payable), and a general read-only role, without access to sensitive information. One way or another, users must be assigned to these roles on an application-by-application basis (and removed from these roles in the event they leave the firm or are assigned to different duties).

There are four reasons this current approach falls short:

1. It is very redundant; assignment to roles and permissions must be executed in many, many places.

2. It is locally idiosyncratic; each application carves up the possible roles differently.

3. It is inconsistent; in most enterprises, the same data exists in many systems. Customer data is typically in dozens of systems (go ask your GDPR implementation project if you don't believe me).

Rules, regulations, and policies about the protection of data are not application specific. In healthcare, the Healthcare Insurance Portability and Accountability Act (HIPAA)—the standards that govern what kind of medical information can be shared—does not suggest you should implement different rules in your Electronic Medical Records system from your Lab System, your Scheduling System, Pharmacy System, or from your Data Warehouse, and yet that is what people do.

4. It is often not granular enough. I had the misfortune to sit in on some of the early planning sessions for HL7's (a healthcare interoperability standard) approach to managing authorization. I watched as they attempted to create roles not only for Physicians Assistants, Nurses, and Doctors (which makes sense at first glance, at least), but then they went on to define roles for all the known medical specialties (and there are a lot). As complex as this was (there were over 100 roles), it wasn't granular enough to address the issues. The core idea in healthcare is what is the relationship of the person accessing the data to the patient (for patient data). It is more important to know whether this is the patient's physician, or a physician in that physicians' practice than it is to know what their specialty.

Given all this, there is a great deal that a generalized, centralized authorization system must do. However, we think this is what makes the model-driven approach even more important.

We need a model-driven way of assigning people to logical roles, rather than relying on people self-selecting roles or being assigned to them by some sort of admin.

The Workers Compensation Insurance company we described was able to assign many users to roles based on their business relationship with the company. If you had a claim, then you were in the injured worker role, which allowed you access to information about your claim (but no others). If you paid insurance premiums, then you were in the role of the an employer, and you had certain access to claim information regarding your employees. If you were an employee of the Insurance company, you were in yet another role.

These roles both granted and denied access (which is one of the reasons self-assignment doesn't work). And they are based on things that change over time (getting injured at work, for instance). If you are both an employee of the insurance company and are injured, you are in a special category (inside claims).

While there is some complexity in this, we believe that a model-driven approach is the only viable way to get consistency and coverage of authorization.

CHAPTER SUMMARY

Model-driven development is not essential in the Data-Centric approach, but the two have some great synergy. When you update your architecture to embrace the Data-Centric approach, you no longer rely on monolithic application software for most of your data management functions. This shift means you have a clean slate for solving common data management issues anew. The model-driven approach is a Data-Centric way to implement common data management functions.

If you adopt a Data-Centric approach, you will often find your model-driven methods easier and more powerful. The "model" part of the model driven approach can stored in the same database, integrated with the Data-Centric model. This makes impact analysis easy. With a traditional system when you change part of the data model you have no idea what code might be affected. When you co-locate your model-driven models with the Data-Centric data model, all the impacts are available through a simple query.

Moving much of what was traditional application logic into the model makes the Data-Centric aspect of the system even more apparent. Moving 90+% of the code to the data models exposes the true algorithms rather than leaving them hidden, marbled in amongst millions of lines of repetitive code.

By merely adjusting how we design and build enterprise applications from an application-centric point of view to a Data-Centric outlook, we can achieve massive reductions in cost and complexity. In the next chapter, we explore how Data-Centric methods can "hitch a ride" on some of the currently emerging technology trends.

CHAPTER 14
Data-Centric and other Emerging Technology

There is a very good chance you will be implementing one of the following emerging technologies, perhaps for a project already underway, or one in the near future.

For each technology, there is a good case to be made that the Data-Centric approach can improve the success of these initiatives.

BIG DATA

Big Data is an approach to data management that is primarily about leaving data where it is, as it is, and sending programs (functions) to the data, rather than trying to homogenize and centralize the data (as would be done in a relational database or a data warehouse).

The classic Big Data approach relies on some sort of parallelizable architecture such as MapReduce or Hadoop.[56] Forrester pointed out that that the implementation of Big Data brought with it the three (and ultimately many more) "Vs.:" Volume, Velocity, and Variety.

- **Volume** is the sheer amount of data. Big Data technology was designed to handle vast amounts of data, up to exabytes of data.

- **Velocity** is the alliterative term for latency; it refers to how long a query or process will take to complete. While Big Data technology could handle huge amounts of data, the approach they took introduced delay. Dispatching thousands of programs, each solving part of a problem and then reconnecting adds a lot of set up time, which impacts big data's use in real-time applications.

- **Variety.** Big Data started life using simple structures (weblogs for instance), but what rapidly happened was a great increase in variety of data formats. This became the central challenge.

---

[56] https://bit.ly/2PikG5H.

Since the initial hype of big data, the pundits have been adding more "Vs," including:

- Veracity (How do you know it's accurate?)
- Value (Can it be applied?)
- Variability (Different sources can be wildly different.)

The net of all this is that Data Scientists are spending 60-70% of their time "wrangling data." A big advantage for data-centrism and big data is pre-organizing and pre-linking the data. Data-centric architecture employs a simple, elegant model. Because of its simplicity, it is easy to conform existing big data to the model; this helps facilitate the process of finding the relevant data.

DATA LAKES

Data warehouses were born of the need to report from many different systems. The data warehouse approach was to create a single data model, that was tuned for common reporting needs, and to populate it with data from many diverse systems. This population process is called ETL (extract, transform, and load). Extract is the process of getting data out of the source system, transform is the process of conforming it to the target data model, and load is organizing it for efficient writing to the warehouse.

While a great idea in principle, it has hardened over time. In most organizations, getting a new dataset into the data warehouse is now a multi-month effort, and sponsors have grown tired.

The confluence of frustration with the data warehouse and big data envy led to the "data lake." The data lake came into existence when people realized that instead of ETL we could just take the source data, more or less as it is, and drop it into a semi-structured data store, and let the data scientists figure it out on consumption.

This, of course, has all the promises and problems of big data, most importantly, that data scientists have to work out what the data means at analytics time. Once again this means that most time is spent finding and understanding the data, and less time is spent with analytics. A further problem for most corporate settings is that the business analyst who could be taught the user-friendly data analytic tools, such as Tableaux, Cognos, and Qlikview is now mostly shut out of participating because of the high bar of skills acquisition needed to access, understand, and work with data in the data lake.

Once again, the Data-Centric approach offers a simple model that the data lake can be mapped to, greatly reducing the time spent finding and understanding problem. We believe that over time there will be more analytics tools designed for business analysts that can directly address this environment.

CLOUD

Almost everyone is moving to the cloud now. On the surface this is neither pro-Data-Centric nor anti-Data-Centric, but it does represent change and opportunity. Many firms recognize that they are making a strategic investment by porting to the cloud. Most can be convinced, at least partially, that the move should be coupled with application rationalization, and a reduction in licensing fees.

Some firms see the move to the cloud as an opportunity to revamp their integration strategy. The most extreme expression of this view occurs when a company moves directly to Data-Centric methods, thereby vastly improving data integration. However, we believe the stampede to the cloud is moving too rapidly to allow something as measured as designing a shared ontology and migrating virtually all of a firm's functionality to it.

Another approach with growing popularity is to use the newer messaging protocols of the cloud, such as Kafka, to provide the excuse to rethink the approach to message-based integration. It is possible to piggyback Data-Centric messaging onto a new initiative like this. By redefining the idea of a canonical message model in semantic and Data-Centric terms, a seed has been planted.

The semantic/canonical model has immediate value in its own right. It drastically decouples applications from each other and ends point-to-point integration. At the same time, its existence provides a safe springboard for re-implementing portions of, or even entire applications.

NLP

Natural Language Processing has been around for a long time. For most of that history its highest value was in "named entity recognition" and "topic identification." Named Entity Recognition is the ability to scan unstructured text and find people, organizations, places, dates, events, and products. These are the "named entities." They are fairly easy to recognize and are somewhat useful to extract.

The next phase of NLP concentrated on identifying "topics," in other words, what is this article about. These became automated "tags" to put on an article.

NLP has also been used to detect "sentiment" in a chunk of text. Is this comment positive or negative? Is the author angry or upset? NLP can help answer these questions.

Only recently has NLP come to the point where it can really contribute to a Data-Centric architecture. The first way is through the harvesting of assertions as triples from documents. As we mentioned, finding the named entities in a document is pretty straightforward. For quite some time, NLP has been able to find people and organizations in documents. Now, though, NLP can identify the relations between them.

For instance, when an NLP system scans a court report, it will easily identify the pertinent lawyers, law firms, plaintiffs, and defendants in the case. The latest cutting-edge NLPs go beyond this, identifying and describing the relationships between the parties (e.g., which lawyer represented which party). With a bit of configuration, this extract process can be conformed to whichever ontology a firm has adopted as the center of its Data-Centric strategy. Suddenly there is a whole new source for data.

The second area where NLP is helping with Data-Centric architecture is extending the core ontology. Some NLP systems are getting good at detecting linguistic clues that suggest classes and/or taxonomic extensions to an ontology. For instance, when an NLP engine encounters a phrase such as "you'll see many types of coniferous trees, such as pine and spruce" it can infer that pine is either a subclass of coniferous tree, or that taxonomically it is a narrower concept.

A third area where we are seeing activity is using NLP to interpret a question asked in unstructured English, translating that to SPARQL, executing it, and returning the results as the answer to the question. So far, we are seeing this primarily in text questions in chatbots and narrow domains, but we expect the domains to broaden and expect to be seeing this capability against spoken questions soon.

RULE-BASED SYSTEMS

Most enterprises eventually need to employ rule-based systems for some of the complex decisions they make on a routine basis. There is an entire industry that caters to this need.

What someone realized at some point was that there were complex business decisions that could either be delegated to humans or could be hardcoded in procedural code. Many realized this was a ripe field for rule-based systems, which can codify the components of the decision process and do it in a way that is non-procedural (i.e., expressed in simple rules that can be combined in ways that would often not have been predicted).

What we have observed is that the "Business Rule" industry has essentially created subroutines for key business applications. Take for example a complex application like insurance underwriting. The core system takes in data (e.g., demographics about the person being insured or their claims history) and then applies "rules" to the data to arrive at a decision. But because of the way these systems have been architected, the rule system is given a bunch of data, and it grinds through a bunch of rules to generate an answer. The answer is returned to the main program that then determines what to do with the advice.

This makes the rule system totally subservient to the vocabulary and API of the calling application. The rule system ends up being captured by the system that is invoking it. This makes it very un-portable. Further the rule system can take no action on its own, it merely returns its conclusion to the calling program, and typically there is no more future for whatever the rule system concluded.

A rule system in a Data-Centric architecture is a peer. This cuts two ways. First, the rule system need not be invoked by any particular process (there can be triggers, or it can run periodically). The most important difference is, rather than just returning an answer to the program that called it, a Data-Centric rule engine persists any conclusion it came up with as conforming triples into the triple store it was attached to. A rule engine that calculates economic order quantities would not be a subroutine to a purchasing application, it would be an independent process that periodically puts data about economic order quantities back into the Data-Centric store. It might calculate, based on purchasing and freight charges, pink pearl erasers should be purchased in lots of 100. This data would be in the triple store attached to pink pearl erasers. Another rule system might independently determine when an order should be placed based on demand patterns, inventory levels, and the new economic order size.

There is a great role for business rule systems in the Data-Centric architecture, but not as most of them are currently configured.

MACHINE LEARNING

Machine Learning (ML) has captured a great deal of attention of late. Systems that can learn a game in the morning and be a world class competitor that same day catch attention.

ML works by processing huge training datasets. Its algorithm pours over the data and using mostly statistical techniques, are able to mimic certain aspects of human thought. But most firms don't have massive datasets; if they do, they're very rarely annotated well. This is one area where it can help to embrace Semantic Technology. There is a subdiscipline of ML called transfer learning,[57] which allows ML to be much more effective with smaller datasets.

The basic idea of transfer learning is rather than use brute force statistical approaches for every problem, sometimes we can use what we've learned in a related domain or problem. Humans do this all the time. We are finding that conforming a dataset to an elegant Data-Centric model reduces the degree of complexity that an ML algorithm needs to deal with. It is complexity that

---

[57] https://bit.ly/2SyjaNm.

drives the need for larger datasets. Additionally, the core data model provides a narrowing and reduction in the hypotheses possible, further reducing the need for large training sets.

The number one reason that established firms are reluctant to adopt ML is its "black box-ness." While ML has had a number of notable successes, how it comes to the conclusions it does, in almost all implementations, is opaque. Very few ML systems can introspect or explain how it came to the conclusions it did. This has led to the dark side of ML, algorithms that reinforce stereotypes, that institutionalize bias, and the famous Microsoft chatbot that rapidly became a profane misogynist.

The Semantic Technology aspect of Data-Centric has a rich history with the "explain function." It was called "proof" in the standards, referring to the mathematical discipline of showing your work as "proof." In Semantic Technology, all inferences are backed up with an explain function that describes how the system came to that conclusion. We think this rich history can be grafted onto the machine learning issues around helping people introspect the models.

MICROSERVICES

The Microservices Architecture movement marries the original goals of object-oriented with the web's RESTful architecture.

The original idea of object-oriented architecture was that there would be a lot of self-contained objects that coordinated with each other to get work done. Unfortunately, virtually all implementations of this idea required that the objects that were interacting be compiled into a single monolithic program that had these characteristics. But a single monolithic system with coordinated self-contained objects is still monolithic. And many of the early object-oriented systems were very monolithic.

While object-oriented was fading in importance (although it never really went away, and most development now is object-oriented), the web was rising in ascendency. The web is built on a very decentralized and loosely coupled model. Reverse engineering why the web was so successful in his 2000 Ph.D. dissertation,[58] Roy Fielding described the primary architectural pattern that the web employed as RESTful, which stood for REpresentational State Transfer. Essentially the web is a bunch of loosely connected endpoints that adhere to a very small number of methods, such as GET, PUT, and POST.

The microservices movement recognized that many of the fine-grained functions that object-oriented wanted to share could be delegated at a much broader scale. Instead of limiting the sharing to modules that were compiled together, microservices made them RESTful dynamic

---

[58] https://bit.ly/1bgKee2.

calls that anyone (typically within an enterprise) could call.

We believe in a well-designed architecture, there will be many dozens to hundreds (but not thousands) of microservices that could be consumed by any use case or process. A service might be, "send a message," "convert an address to geocodes," or "convert a measure in one unit of measure to another."

These services could play a key role in a Data-Centric architecture. The impressive thing is that there are relatively few of them that would cover most of the landscape of services needed for an enterprise.

KAFKA

Kafka is an open source messaging approach that is gaining considerable momentum in enterprises these days.

Many architects are looking at it as one more chance to seize an opportunity that slipped by in the SOA /ESB trend of the last couple of decades. SOA (Service Oriented Architecture) and ESB (Enterprise Service Bus) were more or less synonyms. They each were architectures that advocated a peer-to-peer relationship between applications, mediated through messages that were managed through queues.

At the time (the 1990s and early 2000s) it was felt that it would be unworkable to have enterprise applications communicate directly with each other through cross network APIs. Instead, it was believed that a system of managed queues was what was needed. Changes in one system could be packaged into a message and shipped off to other systems who wished to subscribe. The publishing application need not know how many other applications were interested in (and therefore subscribing to) the changes that they published. Each consuming application had a queue and consumed the messages at their leisure. The publishing application was unaware of, and certainly was not going to wait on, the eventual downstream consumption of the messages.

This was actually a pretty good architecture, and many products were sold that supported it. The reason the concept did not take hold was that instead of creating a common model and common messages that all applications were obligated to conform to, most enterprises took the lazy way out and allowed each application to define their own messages for the ESB. They took the APIs they already had, which were expressed in their own local dialect and structured and published them to the ESB. This meant that any consumers of messages on the ESB had to understand and deal with however many endpoints there were that were publishing similar information. While this homogenized the delivery format, it did nothing for the unconstrained variety that existed in the many source applications. Most firms eventually gave up on SOA and ESB because it did not deliver up to its promise (and this was due to lack of discipline in that it did not address the data variety problem).

Kafka is the new approach to message-based coordination between applications. It offers many things that SOA and ESB did not. It is free, stream based, and much more in line with internet approaches, including a compressed format that combines self-describing data with a smaller payloads (AVRO).

We believe that Kafka is an opportunity to get inter-application messaging right, in the same way that SOA and ESB were. Most Kafka implementations will fall far short of their potential. They will work in the same way that SOA and ESB implementations worked, but they will fall short of their potential in that they will fail to reduce the inter-application complexity.

The big opportunity with Data-Centric methodology and Kafka is to use the core model as the *lingua franca* for the Kafka messages. Firms that base their Kafka messages on a shared core model will find the elusive benefits.

INTERNET OF THINGS

The Internet of Things (IoT) is the term for the next wave of connectivity: where every smart device has its own internet IP address. There are smart controllers in factories, cars, and appliances, but most of them are not connected to the internet. They are primarily connected to very local networks if they are on any sort of network at all.

This is changing rapidly. One of the more visible examples are devices, such as Nest, now owned by Google, which makes some home environment management functions available via the internet. This is poised to explode. Projections are all over the place (billions to trillions of connected devices) but the consensus seems to be that there are already billions of devices connected and in the next 3-4 years there will be tens of billions.[59]

The variety and complexity of these devices is staggering, and therefore the possibility for runaway data complexity is a potential. There is some good news, there are many standards organizations working on standardizing the interfaces. The bad news is that there are many standards evolving, which will, at least for the medium term, contribute to complexity.

Individual organizations can take control of this complexity without waiting by adopting some Data-Centric approaches. While there are an almost endless number of device types that will be connected, there are a fairly small number of things they will do. IoT devices are either sensors or actuators or both. That is, they can either read out some value in the real world or they can

---

[59] https://bit.ly/2kVkk9A.

respond to an internet directed signal to change something in the real world. There are many dozens of things a sensor could detect but depending on your organization, you may only be interested in a small subset.

The Nest, for instance, is a sensor that primarily detects temperature. Its primary actuator turns a furnace or air conditioner on. It has additional sensor capabilities, such as detecting motion, and additional actuators that can be custom implemented, such as those that can turn on a light or open a window.

In an enterprise setting, users may be more interested in greater detail (including electric current fluctuations, humidity, or the presence of various other chemicals). Actuators will break circuits, open gates or doors, or send alerts.

Instead of seeing the IoT as a whole new system, the Data-Centric approach sees how it fits in with and extends the broader business model. A Data-Centric approach to IoT recognizes that the devices in the IoT network are the same devices that are in the asset inventory. The buildings in the IoT are the same buildings that are in the facilities systems, HR systems, and many others. In other words, Data-Centric development is an opportunity to prevent new "silo-ization" of data.

SMART CONTRACTS

Blockchain is all the rage now. Unfortunately, we haven't found a use case in the most visible of the blockchain implementations: the cryptocurrency marketplace. There may be a play there, it just hasn't occurred to us yet.

What has occurred to us is another use case for Blockchain, which is smart contracts. A smart contract is one where key provisions of the contract are coded in a way that can be automatically executed when the stipulated events occur.

In the absence of a shared data model, the participants to the smart contract are reduced to agreeing on what some code will do. By creating a shared model of contract provisions, the participants in a smart contract can define the specifics of the contract, parametrically (essentially a model-driven contract) commit this to the blockchain and have the consequences of the contract executed when the triggers occur.

CHAPTER SUMMARY

New technology will continue its relentless march. If we are not intentional about it, new technology initiatives will compete with funding and attention that could be applied to moving forward on the Data-Centric agenda.

Luckily, pretty much all the trending new technology initiatives can be turbocharged with Semantic Technology and Data-Centric principles. Our recommended strategies are not to compete for funding with these initiatives, but to use their funding to advance the Data-Centric initiative.

Depending on when you are reading this, there may be newer emerging technologies, but a lot of the same thought process should still apply. Depending on which initiative is getting funded, you may have slightly different strategies.

Some initiatives, such as the move to the cloud, are major projects that will touch many or most of your applications. Most firms want to use the move to improve their overall economics, and they know, at some level, a mere "lift and shift" strategy of moving from on-premise to the cloud isn't where most of the value will be gained. The act of rewriting applications is a great opportunity to get at least some of them right in the transition.

Other technology initiatives gain direct benefit from Data-Centric methods; combining them with Data-Centric practices will generally lower their overall cost. Big data and data lakes benefit from adding Data-Centric approaches and thereby aiding data scientists and analysts in finding and organizing the data they are dealing with. Rule-based systems, coupled with Data-Centric, benefit directly by reducing the number of terms that the rules must be written to; NLP and Machine Learning benefit by creating targets for their extraction and by reducing the size of the training sets needed. Smart contracts and IoT benefit from the rationalization of contract terms and reducing the multitude of sensors and actuators to a few simple types. Finally, message and API-related technologies, like Kafka and microservices, benefit from reducing the surface area of their interfaces.

CHAPTER 15
Assess Your Starting Point

If you're still reading, I will assume:

- You are frustrated with the inflexibility and diseconomy that decades of application-centric development have left us with.

- You accept the potential of the Data-Centric approach to reverse most of these trends.

- You are considering at least a partial model-driven future.

- You recognize some emerging technology that you might hitch your projects to.

- The case studies have created some proof that this approach can be brought to fruition.

Now, hopefully, you are wondering, "how can I get started?"

First understand that the transition to data-centrism is a journey, not just a few isolated projects. We believe that the journey starts with taking an objective assessment of your current situation.

Generally speaking, you'll need to:

1. Get a frank assessment of where you stand now. This will include quantifying areas that can be improved.

2. Create a long-term road map. This will be a long-term transformation project. It won't cost a lot, and after the first year or two the project will be funding itself, but it needs some consistency of support to thrive.

3. Look for opportunities to jump-start the change process.

ACCESSING YOUR CURRENT SITUATION

This section is a bit long, but we think pretty essential. A detailed assessment of where you stand now will dispel any Pollyanna beliefs that you are already well on your way—unless of course, you are. We know a few firms that have made considerable progress on their own, but such firms are the exceptions.

Doing a detailed assessment will turn over a lot of rocks. Under some of those rocks will be opportunities that you can use to slingshot your transformation forward.

The other thing a detailed assessment will do is provide the metrics needed to stay the course. When you can start measuring tangible improvements that are coming from your architecture, it will be far easier to continue funding it.

INITIAL SELF-ASSESSMENT

This self-assessment is available on our web site at: https://semanticarts.com/assessment/.

This will give you objective feedback on your responses. Ideally, several people in your firm would perform the assessment for a consistent read.

DATA-CENTRIC SELF-ASSESSMENT

The following are the questions from our self-assessment, along with their rationale.

Question	Implication
When you realize the functionality of your current systems is inadequate, is your first inclination to replace it with another package?	The knee-jerk reaction of thinking first about a package is one the key indicators that your firm is not thinking in a Data-Centric fashion. 0 points for yes, 10 points for no.

Question	Implication
Do you have a single well-defined system of record for each of your major data entities?	A "yes" answer here is a plus for data-centrism. Firms that have identified their "golden sources" are at least thinking in a data-first manner. They may not yet have their systems organized around the data, but at least they know where they are. 10 points for **yes**, 0 points for **no**.
Do you use the phrase "let's not reinvent the wheel" to justify buying a packaged application?	This is a further amplification of question 1 (0 points for yes, 10 points for no)
Can application functionality come and go without requiring a data conversion?	Most companies have built their architecture with application functionality tightly bound to applications, which in turn "own" their data models. Changing functionality means data conversion. 10 points for **yes**, 0 points for **no**.
In the act of implementing a system, do you assume that the existing data has to be converted to the new system?	If you can envision a new system implementation without a data conversion, you are well on the way to being Data-Centric. 0 points for **yes**, 10 points for **no**.
Can different departments have quite different user interfaces and workflows for the same functions?	The only way this is possible is to have an extensible model; this is very difficult without using model-driven development. 10 points for **yes**, 0 points for **no**.

Question	Implication
Do you believe them when your systems implementers tell you there will be a huge "data cleanup" project in addition to your data conversion because of the quality of your data?	"Data cleanup" usually means the new system has arbitrarily different data constraints, and not necessarily that your existing system was "bad." A lot of legacy systems do have severe data quality problems, but often the data cleanup is less for the quality of the code than for its conformity. 0 points for **Yes**, 10 points for **no.**
Do you have a single set of security/authorization rules that are applied consistently to data regardless of its source?	If you have this in place, you have given a great deal of thought to separating your data from the applications in which it is housed. This can be leveraged as you build your Data-Centric architecture. 10 points for **yes**, 0 points for **no.**
Are you spending more money on systems integration (without necessarily having very well integrated systems) than you do on new system functionality?	Most people are. The good news is this may be your motivation for making the switch. 0 points for **Yes**, 10 points for **No.**
Can you easily integrate structured and unstructured data in the same query?	Many people consider this a "holy grail." If you have achieved this goal, some major aspect of your architecture must be Data-Centric. 10 points for **yes**, 0 points for **no.**

Most firms who are not yet on a Data-Centric path score 10 to 30 points. A perfect score of 100 points would represent a firm that has completely embraced the Data-Centric approach. Firms scoring over 70 points are considered Data-Centric, and well on their way to a fully mature environment. We discovered the S&P case study when they took this quiz online and informed us that they had scored 80 points.

ECONOMIC ASSESSMENT

The next thing to do is a high-level information economic assessment. You can start with asking, "How much are we spending on information systems?" Depending on your industry, at a macro level, you are likely spending in the range of 3-10% of your gross revenue on Information Systems.[60]

Industry	IT Budget as a Percent of Revenue
Financial Services	10.5
Government	7.8
Education/nonprofit	6.2
Health Care	5.0
Wholesale and Retail	3.9
Manufacturing	3.4
Overall Sample	6.7

If you are a $1 billion company, you are likely spending $50 million a year on your information systems. This is what you have to work with. As one of our clients says, this is "the size of the prize." The rest of this section is

[60] https://bit.ly/2XuDCB9.

about getting more precise and working out in your
organization where the cost drivers really are and what
the initial opportunities are.

INVENTORY

One of the first inputs you need is an exhaustive
inventory of your systems and databases. If you are a
large company, this very likely exists somewhere, and
you just need to tap into it. If you are a medium to small
company, you may have to take this on yourself. It's not
as hard as it sounds. Your IT department knows the
main applications.

We worked for a State Agency that was concerned about
the number of their applications and the complexity of
the interfaces between them. They shared with us what
they called their "spaghetti diagram":

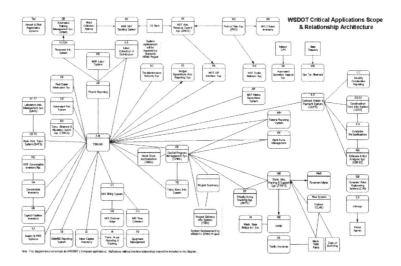

We strongly suspected this was just the tip of their under-documented iceberg of complexity. This State required all agencies to have a portfolio, which was a report describing all their applications. This portfolio contained the name, description, and key characteristics, such as technology, platforms, and number of users. It also contained a section with key interfaces to other systems. We were able to extract this information and put it in a database from which we drew a picture (a complex one, to be sure, but a very helpful picture).

This is an extremely shrunk version of the 12 foot by 4-foot wall chart of their applications and their relationship to each other. The systems from the spaghetti diagram were shown in this diagram and shaded so that people could see how they related to the many other systems that were uncovered.

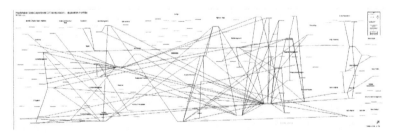

Whether you have the fortune of starting with a portfolio or not, once you construct a first version, the developers and maintainers of the system can help you a lot at this point. What we've seen is the developers and maintainers become very fascinated seeing a picture like this for the first time. Spread this out on a large conference table and invite them in, 4 or 5 at a time.

They will point at the lines, have discussions, disagree with the lines as drawn, "remember" other interfaces not shown. At this State agency, we added so many lines we had to color code them just to be able to follow the lines across the wide expanse of the drawing. They ended up calling the resulting diagram "the spider web on crack":

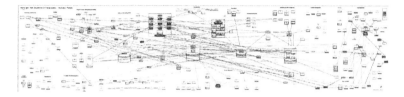

It was actually somewhat readable at full scale. Either way, it makes graphically clear what the issue is: any change to any system potentially reverberates through the interfaces and into other systems.

Getting a full inventory of systems interfaces is much harder than it sounds, but the more you can do here, the better. Most of your spending and most of your lock-in is in these interfaces. Sooner or later, you will need to tackle these if you are to make progress.

The other thing that you will want to do is attempt to inventory "rogue IT" or your "shadow systems." These are the Microsoft Access-based systems and the Excel spreadsheets that are complex enough to be systems on their own. These are harder to find. They can be found by scanning all the drives attached to your network, but you will get a huge number of false positives. You will find thousands of copies of "Northwinds," the sample database that comes with Microsoft Access. You will find thousands of trivial spreadsheets that are neither helpful to nor dependent upon corporate data.

If your company is subject to the Sarbanes Oxley Act of 2002 (often referred to as "SOX"), see if there have been any studies about information provenance. SOX was meant to ensure that companies could trace all the figures on their financial statements through the many processes and programs they went through to get there. Such inventory is the raw material of the "getting better" plan. It is almost certainly the case that few of these systems are sharing databases, but it is also almost certain that they are sharing concepts.

Your goal, which you can measure progress toward, is to reduce the number of applications that are not sharing a core data model. Getting from 1000 applications to 500, even if you make no progress on a shared model, is progress. You will have freed up costs and resources.

As you migrate toward the Data-Centric architecture, you may increase the total number of applications. But having a large number of very small applications that are not interfaced with each other except through the shared model is a completely different economic situation. This is why we suggest counting the number of applications that are not sharing a core model.

PROFILE

The other thing you will want to do is inventory your data, which is even more of a challenge. If you are a billion-dollar company, you could easily have a million data elements under management. You might have a metadata repository (i.e., one place where you are managing the definition of all that data), but it won't be of much use to you. It is too hard to try to understand what a million data elements represent. Metadata typically comprises small amounts of descriptive data, about what each data element means.

Unfortunately, in reality, metadata is often sparse and trivial. For instance, the metadata definition for a column called "order date" might just say, "This is the date of the order." Of course, this isn't particularly helpful, as it hasn't given us any additional details. More useful metadata could specify whether this is the posting date, the effective date, or whether the date that triggers some commitment. Furthermore, this type of documentation (if it is present at all) won't tell you whether the field is in use, or whether it is static or changeable. The names of data elements are often quite cryptic.

Perhaps counterintuitively, looking at the *actual* data can tell us a great deal more than the metadata. There is now software that can help considerably with this. GlobalIDs, Eccenca, and IoTahoe all provide software that interrogates the actual data and profiles what it finds. These profiles are incredibly useful. The first thing they do is eliminate all the elements you no longer need to consider. Any element that isn't used or isn't different is adding no new information.

A second thing these profiling tools do is generate a histogram for each column in each table. The histogram is a summary count of the frequency of data values by column. A column that has exactly one instance per value is likely a primary key, or some other uniquely identifying attribute, such as Social Security Number. If two columns in different tables or different databases share the same histogram, they are very often referring to the same thing. From there the products differ a bit but can include making a first cut assessment of the probable semantics of the data. This can drop the analyst's mental load by a factor of ten.

PROJECTS IN FLIGHT

Find the projects that are in progress, and create an independent assessment of where they stand, how likely they are to complete, and what their net benefit will be if they do complete. We know of at least one firm who took the budget that was already committed to inflight projects and convinced management that they were taking the firm away from their strategic direction. They canceled the projects and reallocated their funds. This freed up funding to start a process to make progress. This is a difficult call to make but can be quite powerful.

SPOTTING AN OPPORTUNITY

Along the way, you will no doubt encounter some projects that will provide quick wins and could be used to bootstrap your Data-Centric initiative.

Additionally, you may come across projects in flight that are not candidates for being cancelled but that might benefit from a Data-Centric approach.

As discussed in the previous chapter, a great place to find opportunity is within trending technologies. Just look at a list of emerging technologies, figure out which one is either already funded or due to be funded, and reframe it with a Data-Centric spin. Virtually all emerging technology benefits from the Data-Centric approach. The trickier part is getting the sponsors of the project to agree.

A SMALL CORE

In addition to finding a project (or projects) to initiate your move to a Data-Centric approach, you should establish a small core team. The function of this team will be to continue to make progress between projects, ensuring that gains achieved are not lost.

All of the successful case studies we have seen employed a small core team with a long-term commitment. Generally, there will not be a lot of turnover on these teams because the kind of people they attract are missionaries. They are typically convinced of the value of this approach and will persevere to get it accomplished. The risk is more that funding or budgets will dry up or that reorganization will disrupt them.

Your job is to find a way to isolate them from the quarter-by-quarter vagaries that so beset most firms. There are many ways to do this, but each is peculiar to the specific company. In some firms attaching this initiative to Enterprise Architecture is safe; in others, a strong data management or data governance discipline can be a good place; for others still, the Chief Data Officers staff is the place. In any event, it is a relatively small but important budget line item, typically being between 3 and 8 people.

GETTING TO SELF-FUNDING

This is a long-term endeavor that only needs a modest investment to deliver superior results over a long period of time. Many firms are currently organizing their IT spend into three categories:

1. **Run the Business:** What do we need to do to keep the lights on and keep the systems working? This is by far the largest portion of the budget, typically 60-70%. The intent is to fund the transform tasks from cost improvement via run-the-business tasks.

2. **Grow the Business:** These are activities or projects that are expected to increase revenue or profit.

One strategy will be to use some of this funding to implement and convert to the Data-Centric approach.

3. **Transform the Business:** These are projects that fundamentally change the way IT and/or business is conducted. We submit that Data-Centric is perhaps the most fundamental of the revolutionary changes. Most strategy firms recommend about 10% of the IT spend be devoted to transformative projects.

Some transformative initiatives are changes in the business model or the way that value is delivered. Examples of major transformations include Netflix's shift from DVDs to streaming, Box's shift from consumers to enterprises, and Tesla's shift from low volume, high-cost cars to high-production, mass market cars. Most firm's legacy infrastructure will frustrate their ability to make such changes.

We contend that the move to Data-Centric is a meta-transformative initiative. By transforming the way IT supports the enterprise, you fundamentally change the enterprise's ability to change itself. Along the way, the move to Data-Centric pays for itself by radically dropping the cost of change, the cost of integration, and the cost of adding new functionality. Data-centric methods reduce cost while they make initiatives to grow the business more effective.

Strategically, you want to make small investments in the transformation that continually funds growth projects and drops the cost of running IT. This chart outlines a representative example.

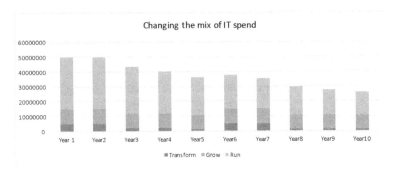

In this example, we start with a modest capital investment to kick start the Data-Centric transformation in years 1 and 2. The continued spend on transformation is maintaining the core team that will support and extend the Data-Centric architecture. In this example, we have left the grow-the-business funding constant. We would expect most grow-the-business initiatives to also be Data-Centric; as such, they should deliver much greater return on investment and much more business impact for the same level of investment.

We show the run-the-business share of IT spending gradually decreasing, as the cost of supporting older integration approaches drops and as functionality previously delivered in expensive legacy platforms is retired and replaced. In most cases, there will be a step function somewhere between years 4 and 8, where there is enough functionality in the architecture, and a track record of implementing in the new architecture, to provide the team the confidence to take on the larger projects. It is not until this point that the entrenched legacy systems can be addressed. We have watched firms attempt to tackle legacy modernization projects head on. Most fail without getting any new functionality implemented. Those few that succeed end up replacing one legacy system with a newer one. Most firms will be better off piling up a series of small wins, building capabilities, skills, and confidence in the new way. By the time they are ready to take on the legacy system, it should be obvious what needs to be done, and rather than launch a large death march project; the firm will launch a series of incremental initiatives.

Finally, in the example, we showed another blip in transformation spend in years 6 and 7. This is meant to represent a true business transformation, which will be possible once the infrastructure has become flexible. It is impossible to predict six years ahead of time the type of transformation the business wishes to do (if it were known now, the business would likely start it immediately despite the lack of infrastructure to support it). The expectation in the graph is that the flexibility in the architecture will encourage business leaders to adopt transformations that they previously would have avoided. By lowering the barriers to transformation, we believe this will encourage them.

Every case we have seen that has been successful has funded a small team for a long period of time. Typically, a team of 3-8 people is all it takes to make this kind of change. They need to be kept in place for a long time. In most enterprises, this means that they need to be delivering incremental value along the way, while they pave the ground for the larger, strategic transformations.

CHAPTER SUMMARY

Preparing the ground is essential here. This is not the kind of initiative to be dabbled with. You need to know exactly where you are starting from and establish a strategy for making continual progress toward your vision.

A great deal of this initial effort will be in "knowing thyself" (that is, deeply introspecting the litany of systems and the economics of implementing and maintaining them). Not only will turning over all these rocks bring forward opportunities that may have been overlooked, they will fuel the inevitable economics discussions that will ensue.

You will no doubt come across projects that would benefit from – and, in turn, help kickstart – the Data-Centric movement within your firm. Organize this data and prepare for the implementation phase.

The other thing to do in the "assess and organize" phase is to figure out how you are going to maintain the consistent, small core team to carry your vision to fruition.

CHAPTER 16
Executing Your Initial Projects

Your first project will be pivotal. A success will help others see the potential in the approach. What follows are some suggestions for getting the most out of this first endeavor.

THINK BIG AND START SMALL

One consistently relevant bit of advice is to "think big and start small." Most IT initiatives embrace one axiom or the other, but not both.

Most projects start small. Unfortunately, when "start small" is the only rule you follow, silos are quickly created. In the same way that every application in an application-centric enterprise, creates its own siloed database, "starting small" (as with traditional agile development) each small project tends to create its own data model.

While starting small is generally a good strategy, it is not enough by itself. We need something to unite the small initiatives. We call that the "Think Big" aspect of the approach.

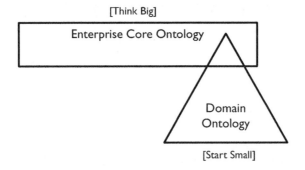

On the other hand, "thinking big" by itself usually results in very grand plans that don't get implemented. This is where the "Enterprise Data Model" came from. Worse than a grand plan that isn't implemented is one that is. Some of the worst debacles in corporate hubris have been the gigantic "think big, implement big" projects. We don't know of any that have succeeded, but we've heard of many failures.

The way we balance these concepts is by having the "think big" portion be limited in duration, but not in scope. We find that it is possible to get a pretty good enterprise ontology for most firms in about three months. The three-month time frame keeps it from being a massive study. Following close on the heels of the ontology is its first application (the think small part). Typically, we're looking for something that can be implemented in a few months, so the scope needs to be pretty small. This combination gives sponsors a great deal of confidence that they aren't investing in a science project.

The first small project may not be ready to go directly into production. The functionality will only be built toward the end of the three-month sprint, and there won't have been enough time to procure infrastructure and the like to take it into production. In many ways, it is a demonstration or an experiment, but as we caution below, it is good to avoid labeling it a "Proof of Concept."

By building the "small" in the context of the "big," we avoid creating another silo. We also can test out key parts of the "big."

ENTERPRISE ONTOLOGY

The core of the "think big" portion is creating an enterprise ontology. Most people have given up on the idea of any sort of enterprise data model, as their history has told them that these efforts are expensive and not useful.

We think the key is to get the maximum amount of coverage with the fewest number of concepts in the enterprise ontology. What we mean by coverage is as you subsequently detail out specific subdomains or applications the hope is that the specific concepts in the subdomain are specializations that were defined in terms of the concepts in the enterprise ontology. Whenever we come across a concept in a subdomain that has no logical parent in the enterprise ontology, we call that concept an "orphan." It is inevitable that there will be a few orphans, but each one should cause you to question your enterprise ontology and your design approach. A true orphan will not be discoverable in enterprise queries and will not participate in the overall integration.

The following example is a great illustration of how this works when it works well. Our firm was working on design only in this case, so we did not ever implement the system, but it still provides a more concrete example. We worked with a State Department of Transportation, and you really can't get more concrete than highways. We built their enterprise ontology, which contained concepts including:

WSDOT Enterprise Ontology				
Project	Intersection	Vehicle	Right Of Way	Roadway
Magnitude	Location	Address	Organization	Roadside Feature

Most of those are self-apparent, except perhaps the last. A "roadside feature" is anything permanently attached to the surface of the earth that you could conceivably hit with a car. It includes trees, large rock outcrops, signs, and the like. It does not include dead animals; while you can hit them, they aren't permanently attached. Roadside features must be near enough a roadway that it is likely that they could be hit.

As we started reviewing some of the more specific systems they were managing, we discovered a "fire hydrant" system, which kept track of all the fire hydrants in the state. Almost all Fire Hydrants are near roadways; they aren't of much use otherwise.

The fire hydrant system contained data including names of fire departments, ID numbers of individual fire hydrants, hydrant locations, water flow measurements, and the contact information of people with access to turn hydrants on or off. It turned out that all these concepts had covering concepts in the core. A covering concept is a broader concept, where the detailed concept is a specialization.

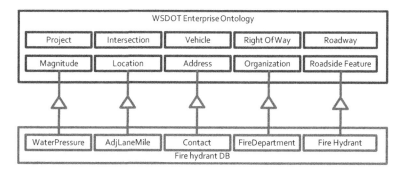

In this example, FireDepartments are specific kinds of Organizations. Their Contact info was specialization of Person and Address, and the AdjLaneMile was a specialization of geospatial information(Location) and would be located on or near a roadway. The flow volume of water is a Measurement, typically in units of cubic feet of water per second. The fire hydrant itself was a Roadside Feature.[61]

Therefore, if someone queried the fire hydrant data using only the enterprise ontology, they would receive *all* the information that was available in the fire hydrant system, without having any prior knowledge of the fire hydrant schema. They would see roadways, latitude, and longitude; they would see organizations and measurements of substances; they would see addresses. They would see a "RoadwayFeature" that was identified as a FireHydrant, despite having no have prior knowledge of FireDepartments, FireHydrants, and perhaps even Water. But the definition of each of these would be just one click away for anyone curious.

GIST AS A STARTING POINT FOR YOUR ONTOLOGY

Establishing a solid Enterprise Ontology early will create a great deal of confidence in the whole endeavor.

---

[61] In the picture and the text, we followed the modeling convention that Classes (sets) are named in "CamelCase" that is initial capital letter, and each word in the name capitalized without any spaces.

Semantic Arts have developed a free "upper ontology" upon which you may base your own enterprise ontology. We call this framework "Gist."

Gist is freely available. It is licensed under the creative commons share alike license and only requires that you post an attribution in your ontology files and that you do not change the namespace. Documentation and the ontology itself can be found at www.semanticarts.com/gist.

We have been building enterprise ontologies for 19 years. Twelve years ago, we began distilling our experience into a shareable base model, naming it "Gist" for the English word meaning "the essence of." Since then, we have used Gist as the basis for every enterprise ontology we have built, in nearly a dozen different industries. We have been refining Gist as well as our methodology for leveraging Gist over this time period such that we now have a great deal of confidence that we can derive an enterprise-specific ontology of very high quality and completeness in a short time frame. We have come up with the term "orphan class" for any new class introduced in an enterprise subdomain that isn't a specialization of a gist class. Or to use our prior term, doesn't have a covering concept in gist. In ten years of working with gist, it has gradually evolved to where most new concepts we encounter do have covering concepts in gist. Our desire to have the ontology be elegant and understandable has led to our continually pruning away concepts that are not essential.

Gist comprises 15 high-level concepts that cover most of the enterprise concepts we encounter in enterprise systems. These 15 high-level concepts are further specialized, making the ontology essentially directly implementable. As of gist version 8.0.0, we now have 127 classes and 119 properties, or ways to connect instances of these classes.

Each industry and each enterprise is different. As such, the concepts and terminology used by Gist must be specialized before it is applied. Regardless, we have found it rare for a finished enterprise core to be larger than twice the size of Gist. Most enterprises have sub-ontologies (we introduced this idea in Chapter 9); each sub-ontology typically adds many dozen more concepts. Even when all the ontologies and sub-ontologies are added up, an Enterprise Ontology derived from gist is still of manageable complexity.

PILOTS, NOT POCS

Many enterprises and vendors have conspired to make doing a "proof of concept" the standard first phase of any project. NASA, perhaps more than any other agency, have made their legacy by moving things from wild idea to standard practice. They created the "Technology Readiness Level," which has nine levels of "known-ness," which in turn shape their approach to contracting.

The levels range from TRL 1, which is for basic scientific research, through to TRL 9, where an actual system has been proven through successful operation.

What we have noticed is vendors tend to like "Proofs of Concept" in that they are to be a first stage in their sales process. If the vendor is selling a product with a high margin, they don't mind that they lose money on these "Proofs of Concept." On the other side, clients have learned that vendors are often all too willing to invest in occasionally elaborate POCs without being funded.

Many mid-level managers in large organizations, without access to budget, found they can do a great deal of very interesting research under the banner of POCs. We heard tell of one mid-level manager at a Financial Services firm who bragged that he had sponsored over 100 free POCs in his career.

At one level this whole Proof of Concept thing seems pretty innocent. If vendors are willing to do them for a chance at a real project, and if clients get value from them, what is the problem?

We became sensitized to the downside of Proof of Concept projects from one of our clients. They were talking internally and had sponsored so many Proof of Concepts (POCs) that they pronounced it "pock." They said they had gotten to the point where they would tell a vendor, "We'd like a proof of concept to see if you can make the sky purple." The vendor would go away for a while, then come back and demonstrate their new sky purpling capability. At this point, the client said, "What are we going to do with a purple sky?"

Around this time, we began to realize that POCs were far less innocuous than we had thought. By focusing on these demonstrations of things that either didn't need to be demonstrated, or that would have no commercial use even if they were real, lead to a lot of wasted time on both sides.

As a result, we concluded that there are very, very few projects that need proof of concepts. Most of the technology that most corporations are going to implement exists and has been successfully implemented by many firms already, so a literal POC in the spirit of a NASA TRL-1-5 is not needed.

What makes much better sense is a pilot. A pilot is a small-scale implementation of a technology that has been proven, but it isn't known how it will be implemented at a particular site. This is very different from a POC. The problem with a POC is even if it is proven, it takes a lot of imagination to figure out how it will be applied to a real business problem. With a pilot, most of the economics have already been worked out. The pilot has a business case, whereas the POC typically does not. The easiest way to tell the difference is to ask yourself: "If this experiment succeeds, will people be eager to implement it?" If the answer is "no," it is very likely it is a Proof of Concept without an attendant business case. If the answer is "yes," you ask, "What do we need to do to roll this out on a broader scale?"

TRUE CONTINGENCIES

If you have found yourself embarking on a large death march project (a project likely to cost $100 million or more, and which statistically is highly likely to fail), you have an interesting opportunity. We call it the "true contingency."

Most projects of this size have a contingency budget. In a triumph of optimism over experience, this budget is usually around 15-20% of the total. Experience strongly suggests that this is not nearly enough. These projects often run over by 50-100% or more. But politically it is impossible to go forward with that range of uncertainty because sponsors of such projects want to be convinced that all the contingencies and risks have been considered.

Given that the contingency is going to be inadequate, and that you are going to blow through it before your systems integrators start with the change orders, it is not really providing you will an actual contingency.

Here is a strategy to consider: take a portion of the contingency and spend it on something that will provide a real contingency. Build a system in parallel in a way that if the primary project gets into financial or technical trouble, the contingent system can be brought forward and put into production.

Most sponsors won't allow you to launch a parallel effort and will question you as to why you think you could implement a system for a few percentages of what the professionals think it will cost. This will require a slight bit of subterfuge. One tack we have been suggesting lately is to say this contingent budget is being spent on a "fully functioning prototype." The prototype idea is that you will want to try out all the user interfaces on the intended users long before you commit to design and code some of the potentially irreversible decisions. The "fully functioning" bit is to make sure this is not just a paper or pretend exercise. You will want realistic (real) data. You will want realistic (real) data volumes. You will want realistic (real) data variability. The most realistic prototype you can build will be one based on the actual data.

If you follow the precepts in this book, you should be able to get this implemented for a small fraction of the main system budget. It will be completely obvious whether it is up to the task or not. In the worst case, you may have wasted a bit of your contingency budget on an effort that may have at least taught you something about your data and your user interfaces.

In the best case, it may save you from catastrophically bad implementation.

CORPORATE ANTIBODIES

An organization is designed, pretty much by accident of birth, for homeostasis. Organizations are like living things in that they are made up of many complex interlocking systems that can take a great deal of perturbation, get knocked about, and return to an even keel. Most of the time, this reliance on homeostasis is a good thing. But when an organization wants to change it finds that the systems that help it withstand threat also prevent positive change.

One of these defense mechanisms we call "corporate antibodies." You've seen these. These are everything from cultural norms to turf battles. A firm will often avoid taking the action it needs to because some people in positions of influence believe the change, while good for the firm, may reduce their power or influence.

> *It should be borne in mind that there is nothing more difficult to arrange, more doubtful of success, and more dangerous to carry through than initiating changes. The innovator makes enemies of all those who prospered under the old order, and only lukewarm support is forthcoming from those who would prosper under the new. Their support is lukewarm... partly because men are generally incredulous, never really trusting new things unless they have tested them by experience.*
>
> Niccolo Machiavelli

Often some manager may suspect that the 100-person project they are initiating may be of marginal to negative value, but they can't resist the allure and excitement of a project of this size.

We have a client who is keenly aware of the politics of organizations. He sponsored an initiative out of his own budget that was a more general benefit to the whole firm. As we were putting the corporate wiki page together, he asked to not have his name as the author or sponsor saying, "Once people start perceiving this as Nic's system they will start resisting it." His advice was that in a large organization, it is often easier to leave a legacy than get credit.

We've seen more good initiatives stall or fail for political reasons than all other reasons combined. Be constantly vigilant.

FEDERATED DEVELOPMENT

We are just beginning to see a new pattern of application development emerging. Rather than copying data from a system of record into the system being implemented (which is the current standard), Federated Development says: let each data owner, each steward, own their data and allow others to access it, as needed.

This is done now in a limited fashion with Master Data Management (MDM) and some API-based development, but these approaches rely on a great deal of programming and coordination.

With data in a standard format (triples), it is possible to construct queries that can combine data from many repositories in one query. This is very difficult to do with traditional technology. It is now possible to federate queries that combine graph data with maps that make existing relational data look like triples and conform to the ontology but only at query time.

Adopting a federated development approach puts you on the road to the end of reconciliations and the end of data conversions.

AN ENTERPRISE KNOWLEDGE GRAPH

Google has popularized the notion of a Knowledge Graph. In Google's case, their graph contains the sum total of everything they have learned by scrapping and re-scrapping the web, as well as from mining your queries, your reaction to your query results, and the effectiveness of all the ads they have placed.

For a firm, the Knowledge Graph is the sum total of what the firm knows, organized around a central model. It comprises the structured data, as well as the myriad bits of miscellaneous "knowledge" captured and organized elsewhere (e.g., in external spreadsheets). With a Knowledge Graph in place, a firm will not only enjoy access to all they know – they will be able to infer more from the information already there.

CHAPTER SUMMARY

Your first few projects will be key to getting a Data-Centric culture established. There is a certain amount of tension between solving the broad firm-wide problems and tackling specific, quick-win projects.

Our advice is to embrace the tension. Start with a first version of an enterprise ontology. Even if it is very thin, it will guide future integration and hold the whole initiative together. At the same time, build out something specific of value. This initial system will often be the integration of several other systems that have been historically hard to integrate. It may be the integration of two types of data, such as structured and unstructured. This is often enough for others to see the value in the approach.

The elegance of your enterprise ontology will be key in keeping the tide of complexity at bay. Your first projects should be examples, existence proof that this new approach is viable and desirable.

We have seen the firms that get off to a good start get results in a short enough time span that they are encouraged to stay the course. Early wins lead to additional investment and each round of success brings you closer to the ultimate goal.

CHAPTER 17
Governance and the New Normal

Soon after your first few successful projects you will need to begin to consider how to pivot to this being the new way to do things. You may find yourself swamped with internal demands and in need of some stabilizers. This section is about how to start the transition to the new normal.

THE NEW APPROACH BECOMES "HOT"

We've seen several variations on this. Sometimes, as with the Standard & Poor's case study, executive management edicts that all other divisions are to adopt the new Data-Centric approach. This can totally overwhelm the small group that was chartered with supporting their own division.

Sometimes, as with an Investment Bank, we've been working with, word gets out that this new approach delivers impressive results, rapidly. New initiatives are launched to replicate the success in other divisions.

In either case, whether by edict or by appreciation, this is what is predictable: there will be projects launched without the requisite thoughtfulness and planning, and these projects will create the equivalent to Gartner's hype cycle. Some of the projects will be launched with the aim of reproducing the results of the first few projects will do so with limited experience and produce disappointing results.

THE EXECUTIVE'S ROLE IN PILOTING THE CHANGE

If you find yourself in the position of the executive who is associated with the change, and therefore for propagating it through the enterprise, you are faced with some tricky positioning. You may be tempted to single thread new projects through your organization, which now has a track record of implementation. But this will be frustrating for two reasons: you will not have the capacity, and others will literally want to do this themselves.

What we have seen to be more effective is to build an internal consortium. This can be modeled on industry consortia. The difference between a consortium and a typical enterprise project, or even typical enterprise governance, is the volunteer nature and the lack of command and control structure. In this case, the consortia can be built around the notion of sharing. This will be sharing and extending models (ontologies) as a way to promote integration; it will also be about sharing actual data. By federating queries and using some shared ontologies, we can finally get past the insane practice where every application has many redundant (but differently structured and named) representations of the same corporate data (e.g., products, customers, orders, trades, vendors, employees, or departments)

Finally, the consortia can come together to share best practices. This is a new undertaking for most enterprises, so there will be many opportunities for learning and reporting on lessons learned.

A KINDER/ GENTLER VOLUNTARY GOVERNANCE STRUCTURE

In many firms, "Governance" has a bad name. It is often seen as a necessary evil, something imposed from on high that you must conform to. It is often blamed for delay and unnecessary bureaucracy. And if you were to suggest that you are implementing "governance" on your own, you will likely get visited by someone from corporate who will inform you, "We can take it from here."

As a result, you may not want to call what you are doing "governance," even though it is. Once you get a few projects in the Data-Centric mold, and you have a consortium in place, people are depending on the stability and availability of the core model. Therefore, you have to have some procedures in place that look a heck of a lot like governance. What these processes will share with traditional governance is a desire to manage change.

> *The art of progress is to preserve order amid change*
> *and to preserve change amid order.*

> Alfred North Whitehead

One of the differences is that in a traditional environment, change is hard. If any change manages to make its way through the budgetary and other hurdles, it must be reviewed to make sure it doesn't break anything. In the Data-Centric world, we are trying to encourage change, and certainly, the technology makes a certain level of change much more feasible.

However, as you can imagine, the combination of higher rates of change plus more integration and dependency does offer up some challenges for governance. The next couple of sections suggest a few techniques that can make things go a bit better.

GOOD, BETTER, BEST

One of the things that happen once this approach becomes dubbed the "new normal" is everyone hops on board and attempts to emulate as best they can, but they really aren't very good at it. This has happened with most of the improvements in IT over the last decade.

The original data warehouse wars were between the Kimball approach and the Inmon approach. Each offered insightful design and guidance on things, such as "conformed dimensions" (ways that data warehouses could share "rollups" for things like geography or product families). I think the lead methodologists for the Data Warehouse movement, Bill Inmon and Ralph Kimball,[62] would be horrified to see what we see in data warehouses now. We have several clients who have data warehouses with thousands of tables. Not much conformance going on there.

The agile movement, described earlier in this book, has many virtues. However, in the wrong hands (and about half of the hands are wrong) it has led to runaway "cowboy coding" (i.e., letting programmers do whatever they want with little direction or accountability).

The Data-Centric approach will no doubt suffer some of these same problems. We already see it. The best we can

---

[62] https://bit.ly/2bCQyCA.

do is offer some guidance that will allow some visibility and a nudge towards doing it right.

The next couple of sections are a few ideas to steer well-meaning, but potentially rogue, groups into the light.

TBox, CBox, ABox

Meaning

In Semantic Circles, the part of the ontology concerned with defining classes and properties (the closest equivalent to schema in a traditional system) is called the "TBox" (Terminological Box), the place where new terms are defined.

Relationships

The "ABox" (Assertional Box) is the term for where the specific factual assertions are made. This is more akin to the instance data in a traditional system. It is the triplication of data.

Categorical

We have introduced a third term and it seems to be quite popular with our business sponsors: the "CBox" (Categorical Box). This is where taxonomies and enumerated lists are defined and managed.

These are slightly awkward terms, but they turn out to be quite useful in governance discussions.

In a traditional system, there is quite a pronounced difference between schema and data. They are expressed in different syntax (DDL (Data Definition Language) and DML (Data Management Language)) and are stored in different places (the catalog, directory version, or the data tables themselves).

In semantic systems, all three of the "Boxes" are expressed as RDF Triples. They can be intermingled in the same repository, or they can be stored separately. However, the three "boxes" represent fundamentally different kinds of things, and it is helpful to have reference labels to distinguish them. This is especially the case when it comes to governance.

The TBox, while numerically simple (that is, we recommend trying to keep the number of concepts down to several hundred for the core enterprise model, and even less than that for each of the subdomains), is quite complex in its actual structure of formal definitions, and the implications for reasoning and inference can be subtle. For this reason, we recommend the TBoxes be governed primarily by trained ontologists and under the guidance of the business leaders who sponsored the terms in the first place. There should be a TBox governance committee for the shared ontology as well as one for each domain ontology.

The CBox is often numerically much larger, with potentially hundreds of categories that have enumerated types, some of which contain thousands of specific categories (the *taxons* in the taxonomies). After some initial setup and guidance, the CBox can and should be managed primarily by the business sponsors. They have considerable expertise in these pursuits and have been managing reference data and taxonomies for decades. There are tools such as SmartLogic, Collibra, TopQuadrant's EVN, and Pool Party that make organizing end user management and governance far easier. These tools also have the added advantage of tying in nicely with the TBox ontology. We recommend the CBox be primarily governed by representatives of the business community who have a stake in their use.

In most cases, there will be some CBoxes that are widely shared and should therefore be governed by a central group; a larger number that are local to a domain can therefore be governed by a local group.

The ABox is typically governed by IT, and much of this is delegated either to the existing applications, or in the future to the constraint and identity management layers of the Data-Centric architecture. There must be a way to continually refresh the ABox assertions, primarily from the databases and datasets that IT manages. They will primarily be concerned with issues, such as consistent URI minting and detecting whether the same referent is being referred to using different IDs in different systems and how to resolve that in the ABox data. ABox governance is mostly about integrity management, versioning, and recency. The ABox governance leaders will also sit on the TBox governance committee, but mostly to get advance warning and weigh in on changes to the TBox that might alter ABox processes.

SHARE THE LEARNING

Transformation is a learning process. The firm has to learn a new set of habits and behaviors. The effectiveness of the transition will turn on how well the firm shares what it is learning as it is learning it. There are multiple strategies for sharing the learning that seem to work well in this environment. What doesn't work as well is traditional governance. Traditional governance assumes that the firm knows the right way to do something and must police it. The firm will be learning as it transitions through the transformation, so better strategies are those that assume and encourage co-learning.

Setting up a community of practice with regular conference calls is one good way to share both the learning and status at the same time. You might be surprised how many people in your organization are already thinking this way and are just looking for some encouragement and a venue. We gave a workshop at a large German firm. They sent out a series of emails to see if anyone was interested in the new "semantic thing" and were surprised to find almost a dozen projects were already in progress (although with little coordination).

DATA-CENTRIC MATURITY

This is an initial outline for a maturity model. I have participated on other collaborations to build maturity models, and I know it takes a considerable amount of coordination, leadership, and commitment. I would be happy to participate in such an endeavor if a firm or consortium were interested in providing the structure and leadership.

Meanwhile, the following should provide an outline of the areas I believe should be covered by such a model. We don't yet have a fully worked maturity model but would be happy to work with anyone who would like to help develop one.

The following general categories seem to cover most of that which we would expect to be important in tracking the progression through a Data-Centric transformation:

- Organization and Policy—is the organization set up in a way to foster the transformation?

- Artifacts—does the organization have the things it needs for success, including an enterprise ontology, a graph-based architecture, training materials, and skilled workers?

- Progress—does the organization have a road map, is there a complete inventory of the current data stores, and has it been analyzed in a way that would promote eventual mapping?

- Results—are pilot projects delivering predicted improvements? Is the overall effort having an impact on the economics of information systems and the business as a whole?

Within each of these, we expect the main subdivisions to be:

- Organization and Policy
  - Funding
  - Executive support
  - Policies
  - Organizational structure

- Artifacts
  - Enterprise ontology
  - Training materials
  - Governance manual
  - Model-driven architecture

- Progress
  - Inventory of existing data stores
  - Datascape understood
  - Datascape mapped
  - Road map
  - Staff trained

- Results
  - Pilot projects hitting target economics
  - Cost of new applications
  - Cost of change
  - Cost of integration
  - Ease of understanding
  - % of available integrated data

The following is how we expect most companies will work through their transformation. Most firms will start with virtually nothing. They will be in the application-centric quagmire (new projects are hideously expensive, change is prohibitive, and integration consumes most of the budget).

The first thing will often be an enterprise ontology with some executive support and perhaps followed by a pilot project.

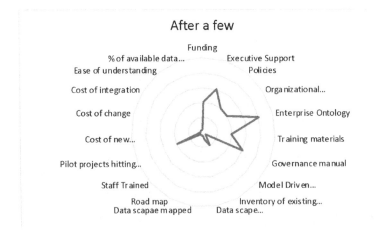

As the idea begins to take hold, many firms will start setting up formal governance structures.

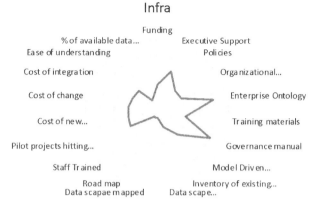

Then it will be time to start investing in infrastructure, both computational as well as organizational.

After a few ad hoc successes and as the firm begins to get on board, it will be time to take stock of the whole landscape.

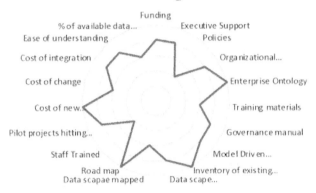

storming

Funding
% of available data...   Executive Support
Ease of understanding   Policies
Cost of integration   Organizational...
Cost of change   Enterprise Ontology
Cost of new.   Training materials
Pilot projects hitting...   Governance manual
Staff Trained   Model Driven...
Road map   Inventory of existing...
Data scapae mapped   Data scape...

Finally, as more and more of the firm converts, the results should become the main thing.

Not every firm will progress through these stages in this order, but this should be at least one reasonable path through the transformation.

CHAPTER SUMMARY

After some initial project successes, you may be lulled into thinking that this is the new normal, but our observation is that firms that have created this approach as the new normal, in addition to executing successful projects, need to set up governance processes to keep the momentum going (as well as to keep future projects between the guardrails).

The key tasks to keeping the momentum going are to set up an appropriate governance program, mechanisms for sharing and propagating lessons learned, and then a measurement program.

The key takeaway for the governance process is to separate governance by type (TBox, CBox, and ABox) as well as scope (Enterprise and Domain).

The key takeaway for sharing is to set up websites, portals, wikis, and forums that allow new groups to benefit not only from the learning of those who have gone before, but also to leverage and reuse the TBoxes, CBoxes, and ABoxes that exist.

The key takeaway of the measurement program is to use key metrics to assess and continually drive toward broader and deeper maturity of the practice.

CHAPTER 18
Wrapping Up

This book covers a great deal of ground. The change outlined here will be profound for the firms that take this on.

Hopefully, we have convinced you that a Data-Centric approach to enterprise information systems is both desirable and doable. We have reiterated the horrible economics of the status quo at most enterprises. We have demonstrated through case studies, and short vignettes that data-centrism is possible and other firms are actively achieving it.

We spent a fair bit of time outlining the power of Semantic Technology and how it can aid you in this endeavor. It is possible, as we saw with the early case studies and by extrapolation, everything we said is needed to implement a Data-Centric approach can be done with non-semantic technology (either traditional technology or NoSQL approaches). We do think that the mental shift that comes with viewing the world through a semantic lens, as well as some of the specific capabilities of Semantic Technology, make this arduous task at least a bit more doable.

We've described some next steps to put you on the right path and that we've already seen work in a number of large enterprises.

All the details can't possibly be captured in this book. Specific guidance on ontology modeling and conforming architecture will be in two upcoming volumes.

The rest you will have to work out as you go. While you won't be the first explorers on this new continent, you will be far ahead of supply lines, and there isn't yet a large industry to help you through.

Someone once said that the highest motivation comes when one is unsure about the success of the outcome of a new venture. If you are 100% certain of the positive outcome of a new venture, you will be bored. If you are 0% certain of the positive outcome (and 100% certain of a negative outcome), you will be frustrated. Uncertainty provides motivation. Venture capitalists and entrepreneurs seem to thrive on very low degrees of certainty. Most of us mere mortals seem to do better in the 70-80% range.

I hope this book gives you the encouragement to start the journey and enough guidance to get your success level up.

You are not alone. I encourage you to join over 500 professionals who have left very thoughtful quotations on our Data-Centric Manifesto page (http://datacentricmanifesto.org/). It is an exciting time to be changing the world. Welcome aboard.

ABOUT SEMANTIC ARTS

Semantic Arts is a professional services firm specializing in helping firms make the transition to becoming Data-Centric. We were incorporated in June 2000 focusing initially on helping firms adopt Semantic Technology.

This gradually led us to the realization that the most profound value of adopting semantics would be in putting it to use in reversing the current trend of information system implementation.

If you would like advice or help with your Data-Centric initiatives, please do not hesitate to contact me at mccomb@semanticarts.com.

ABOUT THE AUTHOR

Dave McComb is the President and co-founder of Semantic Arts. Prior to founding Semantic Arts, he was, as he puts it, "part of the problem." He started his career with Andersen Consulting (the part of Arthur Andersen that eventually became Accenture). In his 13 years at Andersen, he led a number of large, successful enterprise application development projects, including two custom ERP design, build, and implementation projects (one of which took place in Papua New Guinea, one of the remotest places in the world).

He left Andersen to pursue and promote the adoption of what was then the relatively new discipline of Object-Oriented development. It was in this incarnation that he began to see the semantic light. The process of identifying and designing the "classes" in an object-oriented system seemed so arbitrary and unprincipled. Two early white papers[63] [64] provided the impetus to begin viewing information from the vantage point of meaning.

In 1992, while working with the architects who designed all the Wal-Marts in North America, he led his first semantic modeling workshop and began building Object-Oriented systems around a semantic core.

In the mid to late 1990s, while getting his dot com merit badge, he co-founded Velocity.com, which was a

---

[63] Hammer & McLeod "Database Description with SDM: A Semantic Database Model "ACM September 1981 https://bit.ly/2UPpUMp.

[64] Hull & King "A Tutorial on Semantic Database Modeling" ACM September 1987 http://bit.ly/2IPqP8n.

healthcare software startup. One day while drawing a detailed rendition of the architecture on a white board, it occurred to him that lurking in the many configuration files scattered throughout the architecture was a model. This eventually became a semantic model, and not of an application but applications themselves. This led to rebuilding the architecture around this model, which was patented as the first fully model-driven architecture.

Velocity's dot com bubble burst, along with so many others, in the spring of 2000. As the architecture and the patents were caught in the burning wreckage of Velocity.com, he and some of his co-conspirators postulated that what they had learned in uncovering and applying semantics might form the basis for a professional services consulting practice.

Semantic Arts was launched in the summer of 2000. In 2001, the Tim Berners-Lee article[65] in Scientific American hit the newsstands. It looked like it would only be a matter of time before companies were clamoring for Semantic Technology.

It was a matter of time. A lot of time. For most of those early years the crew bid on and performed traditional IT consulting projects (feasibility studies, requirements analysis, long-range IT plans, architecture designs, and the like). Every project was executed using Semantic

---

[65] http://bit.ly/2GmiTZa.

Technology, mostly in the background, occasionally surfacing in some deliverables.

Dave McComb wrote <u>Semantics in Business Systems</u>[66] in 2003 and co-founded the Semantic Technology Conference in 2007. And as Yogi Berra has so famously observed, "They stayed away in droves." Finally, the ice began to melt. Companies began asking for semantics. The "O" word (Ontology) could be uttered in polite company. The firm began building ontologies and designing semantic architectures to implement them. And the ontologies and architectures languished on bookshelves.

The firm pivoted. Semantic Arts needed to become enablers, so they built architectures, loaded the architecture with ontologies, and populated it with triples. As with many software companies they built their own internal systems using the approaches they espoused, in the process known as "eating your own dog food.[67]" By building their own systems with the technology they recommend to clients, they get an early preview of what works and what doesn't work.

Their current primary offering is guiding clients through the transition to the Data-Centric approach.

---

[66] https://amzn.to/2XuJJFz.

[67] "Not Eating Your Own Dog Food? You Probably Should Be" Forbes March 4, 2014 https://bit.ly/2IUFqh2.

Index

Made in the USA
Columbia, SC
05 September 2019